I Told You Not To Climb The Cactus

I Told You Not To Climb The Cactus

Written and Illustrated by

Wendy Hamilton

ZealAus Publishing

I Told You Not to Climb the Cactus

Surviving the Badlands of Motherhood

Second Edition

Copyright © 2019 by Wendy Hamilton
Illustrations © 2019 by Wendy Hamilton

www.zealauspublishing.com

All rights reserved.
No part of this book may be reproduced or transmitted in any form or by any means without written permission of the author.
Some names have been changed to protect identities.

ISBN: 978-1-925888-32-4 (e)
ISBN: 978-1-925888-07-2 (hc)
ISBN: 978-1-925888-08-9 (sc)

Dedication

Thanks to the mothers who have been.
Courage to the mothers who are.
Hope to the mothers who will be.
This is my gift you, the promise
of one who has gone on before.
Do not despair in the task
you find yourself doing.
It is more important than the
world will ever admit.
In your combined hands reside a
thousand different destinies and
all the future of our world.
Be brave and courageous in the
path you are walking, for I have
found that although the road was
hard, the destination was sweet.

Contents

Introduction 1
Monkeys and Magic. 4
New Parents.. 13
The Wounded Ego. 22
Madonna and Child. 28
Socialization. 36
Guerilla Warfare. 39
A Bonding Moment. 50
Telephone troubles.. 55
Kids Clothes. 61
Waifs and Strays. 67
The Transformation. 73
A Good Deal. 77
The Sign Again. 80
Wet Weather.. 86
The Tyrant and the Slaves. 93
Prams, Strollers and Pushchairs. 98
Birth Order Pitfalls. 109
Do Not Climb the Cactus 116
Little Red Hen's Day of Rest. 121
More Rest on Sunday. 128
Fiona and Friends. 135
The Teachable Moment. 142
Life and Death. 151
Four is Quite Enough! 155
Time out.. 160
Running Away. 169
About the Author 176
Other Books By Wendy Hamilton 177

Home Sweet Home.

Wendy Hamilton

Introduction

I make no secret of the fact I would rather sit on the couch and eat chocolates than climb a mountain. That is why I have never climbed the one called Lot's Wife. It towers above my parent's beach house and oozes rugged magnificence. I got there by proxy once, however.

"Take some pictures of the view when you get to the top," I said to my husband Ian as he and my brother-in-law prepared to take all the kids hiking one holiday. "Don't rush, don't hurry home, and wave to us when you get there."

"We will see you from the garden," encouraged my sister Antoinette. She was as thrilled as I was over escaping the ordeal.

"Why would we bother climbing all the way up there when we can get them to take a photo?" I said as we waved goodbye.

"I couldn't agree more," said Antoinette, sipping cool lemonade. "Seriously, who wants to struggle up a steep muddy track surrounded by a pack of yapping kids?"

I Told You Not To Climb The Cactus

"Especially if the alternative is lounging in a deck-chair," I finished, popping a caramel centered chocolate into my mouth.

"*Childless*," said my sister, "you left out the most important part."

"That goes without saying," I agreed.

It was a delightfully lazy afternoon, and I enjoyed every decadent minute. When I saw little figures like lice on the head of Lot's beloved, I felt nothing but smugness. It was not until the evening, when I saw the panoramic photographs of the superb sea and landscape, that my world view crumpled. The men and kids had glowing faces that oozed endorphins. I, however, felt the sluggishness that comes from lack of exercise and too much sugar. By nightfall, I was not so sure I had chosen the best way or been so clever. Their day involved a lot of effort and discomfort, but the end result was a sense of accomplishment. My day was easy, yet it seemed little and shallow in comparison.

Motherhood was another mountain I did not want to climb. I make no secret of the fact I would rather eat chocolates than have a baby. I did, however, (very reluctantly) get out of my deck-chair to give birth four times. The mountain called Motherhood, has been tough going, filled with pitfalls, slithery bits, and seemingly impassable precipices. There were moments when it felt as if I was climbing a cactus. But the view, now I am nearing the end of the climb, is worth it all. Who would have guessed the child with THE MOUTH who drove me nutty with her constant talking, would turn into an elegant woman with keen insight and delightful conversational skills? That the shy one who burst into tears if a visitor looked at her, would travel through pirate-infested seas to work in an orphanage

Wendy Hamilton

in Sri Lanka. That the toddler playing with used diapers, or the baby (that his sister thought was her puppy) would grow into such handsome young men. While it is true, my face is more lined and I never got to eat as many chocolates as my childless friends, I'm glad I got out of my comfort zone and had kids. After all, nothing worthwhile in life comes easily.

I Told You Not To Climb The Cactus

Monkeys and Magic.

An honest man once said, "I wouldn't give you two cents for your child, but I would die for my own."

I understood the first half of his statement. I was not keen on motherhood because it involved children.

"I just don't like them," I said to my mother. "Sticky fingers, runny noses, and all that howling and screaming. I can't stand it."

"Don't make the mistake of looking into prams," said my mother who knew where I was coming from (it seemed the apple had not fallen far from the tree.) "I spent the whole nine months I was pregnant with you, torturing myself by looking in prams and asking *could I love that*?"

We both knew that the answer was no, yet I was a very loved child.

"Your own are different," said another veteran mother, "your own are beautiful."

Wendy Hamilton

"I certainly hope so," I thought. Newborn babies looked like ugly red monkeys. If I followed my natural inclination, I would keep well away from all children. I would rather have an old lady any day. I knew how to relate to the elderly. They moved slowly and only in extreme cases put their clothes on back to front.

So, I put off having a baby. I knew, however, it was unlikely that I would get through life without encountering motherhood, some things happen like it or not. Besides, I had observed that people who never had kids lacked a certain depth, it was as if the nurturing side remained undeveloped. I also noticed that they aged slower and kept youthful faces longer, which seemed ominous. It suggested (as I suspected) that raising kids was a grueling occupation.

As I moved towards the latter end of my twenties (and as my husband did not suffer the same dread of the idea) I realized it was time. The more I read about child-rearing the more nervous I got. I dithered along the pre-pregnancy diving board. The plunge into the deep dark water of motherhood below looked sickening. What scared me was, once I jumped there was no going back.

"It's worse than deciding to get married," I moaned to Ian. "It's a lifelong commitment and I don't know if I can do it?"

"You took the risk and married me," said Ian.

"Yeah, but I got a good look at you before I purchased," I objected. "Kids come in brown paper bags with a large *no return* scrawled on them." I picked up the cat and buried my head in his fur.

"You'll be alright," said Ian, "a baby is like a cat."

I was not so sure about that. I was much less afraid of getting a cat than having a baby. When I was a child, I had

I Told You Not To Climb The Cactus

stumbled across my mother's diary. *Having Wendy was a nightmare* I read. A nightmare; that did not sound good. I did not want to go through a nightmare of pain.

"No, the pain wasn't a problem," said my mother when I finally admitted to her that I had read her diary. "It was the Matron. She was an old battle-ax and I was frightened of her. Thank goodness hospitals don't have old tartars like her anymore."

That was a relief. Giving birth in the 1960s sounded horrible. No husband in those days entered the delivery room and babies slept in the hospital nursery. The protocol surrounding childbirth was much more humane in the nineties.

Getting pregnant once I took the plunge, was quick. It was as if God knew I would change my mind if I had to wait. Surprisingly, once the doctor confirmed a baby was on the way, most of my jitters disappeared. Some bits were even pleasant.

"It's fun collecting baby clothes," I said to my sister who took a great interest in the growing bump. "I love knitting booties and bonnets they make me feel clever."

"I've brought you a present for the baby," said Antoinette, "It's in the car. "Ooo, how exciting," I said levering my bulk out of the chair I was sitting in.

"It's second-hand you'll have to do work to it," she cautioned as I waddled behind her.

"Sounds more and more interesting."

"What do you think?" she asked, throwing open the backdoor of her car.

"I love it," I said peering in at the framework of a cane bassinet. "It's got drapes but they are tired looking," said Antoinette gathering up a bundle of pink cloth.

6

Wendy Hamilton

"I can easily replace them," I said fingering the faded fabric. "I'll use these old ones as a pattern and replace them with white lacy ones."

We hauled the bassinet out of the car and carried it into the house.

"I think my nesting instinct must be strong," I said to Antoinette as I made us a cup of tea. "I love all this preparation."

"That's good," said Antoinette tying the old drapery on the bassinet so I could see how it looked.

"Yes, but it makes me worry."

"Why?"

"It highlights a lack of maternal feelings," I admitted, lifting tea bags out of our cups. "My bump doesn't seem like a baby." I handed her a steaming cup before easing myself into an armchair. "I need a big dollop of hormones when this baby arrives or I am in trouble," I continued, as I balanced my tea on the shelf of my stomach.

"Have you been looking into prams again?" asked Antoinette.

"Yes," I admitted, peeling a banana.

"Don't you remember what Mum said?"

"Yes, I know. I try not to, but sometimes I can't help it," I said scoffing down the banana. "Toddlers are the worst; filthy faces, stinking bottoms, and howling mouths."

"Ooo you're right," agreed Antoinette. My sister's apple fell from the same tree. "Disgusting. Don't ever say give *Auntie Antoinette a kiss* if it is covered with chocolate," she added shuddering.

"I will never do that to you," I promised. "I had been on the receiving end of that dubious treat a few times myself. Why do mothers do that?"

I Told You Not To Climb The Cactus

The bump had grown.

"Beats me," said Antoinette. "I'm glad it's you that's having a baby and not me."

As much as I enjoyed my sister's empathy, I needed to look elsewhere for reassurance.

"I still don't have any maternal feelings," I admitted to Ian. By now the bump had grown to the size of a watermelon. "I suppose, I am balancing my cup just above the baby's bottom, but it seems more like a small table, I said putting a plate of sandwiches next to my tea.

"You'll be right," said Ian unconcerned. "Have you been looking in prams again?"

"Yes," I admitted. "I try not too but I can't help myself. The toddlers are the worst."

"You're not having a toddler."

"Not at first," I said darkly, "but babies grow into toddlers."

"You'll feel differently when it arrives," predicted Ian breezily.

"I'm getting awfully close to my due date," I said nervously. "There should be some maternal feelings by now. Other women get all goo-gar and melty when they see babies."

"Well you still have time. You're not due for a few days yet."

"I suppose," I said hopefully.

But on the morning my baby was expected, the maternal feelings were still absent. At the end of the day, they were not the only thing missing; the baby also had not turned up.

"That was an anticlimax," I said looking at my bag of baby clothes. The lack of activity after a forty-week countdown was disconcerting. I felt like I had lit a skyrocket and the fuse had blown out. The departure date had come

I Told You Not To Climb The Cactus

and the ship had sailed without me. "I'm not having a baby at all," I told Ian as I lumbered about the room. It was a silly thing to say yet it felt like the absolute truth.

"The baby will come when it comes," said Ian. He was right of course. It took another week, however, before things started happening.

"I think I'm in labor," I said shaking my husband awake. I had left him to sleep as long as I could.

"How far apart are your contractions?" he asked catapulting out of bed.

"I'm not sure," I admitted. I lumbered over to an armchair in the tiny lounge of our rented house and plunked down. I found sitting up was the most comfortable position. Another contraction hit me. It felt like a bell curve. A small pain gathering in momentum until the crescendo then tapering down to nothing again.

I closed my eyes, relaxed and rode the wave like a surfer.

"Thirty seconds," said Ian when I opened my eyes. He rushed into the front bedroom. I could hear him rattling about in the drawer of his desk. When he came back, he was clutching an old math's book. He threw himself on the floor by my feet and rolled onto his stomach. He spread the book open, drew the axis of a graph and marked a dot on the appropriate spot.

I closed my eyes and rode the wave of another bell curve, which Ian charted with a dot on his graph.

It was very peaceful sitting there in the dim room. The only light was the street lamp shining through the window. Ian's actions were so him, it was reassuring. His presence was as good as a pain killer. If he left the room for even a few minutes, the pain spiked.

"I think it is time to call the midwife," I said to him at

five in the morning. "I feel the need for someone who knows what they are doing. The contractions are getting bigger."

"Good idea," said Ian looking at his graph. "They are also closer together."

Linley the midwife, arrived shortly after Ian's phone call. She was warm and friendly, very different from the matron of Mum's diary. She looked at Ian's chart and checked my progress.

"I think it is time to go to the hospital," she said.

"I wrapped my bathrobe tighter and tied the belt as best as I could around my huge stomach. The bump still did not seem remotely like a baby and I still lacked maternal feelings; perhaps they would show up when we got to the hospital I thought, as the wheels of the car spun along. But alas, they were absent at the swing doors of the maternity department, and all the paperwork in administration did not help. Even the delivery room, merely underscored how absurd the idea was, of the bump traveling from me to the Perspex crib.

The whole process was getting very tiring. I wanted to go to sleep, but it was impossible; especially in transition when the contractions rolled continuously like waves in a storm. Right at the end it got a bit much.

"Breathe in," said Linley putting a gas mask over my face.

I took a deep breath and floated away pleasantly; shortly after, Marie was born.

It is easy to lose sight in the drama of childbirth, that all the activity has an end goal; at least it is until they put your baby in your arms.

As I held my firstborn, the magic dust of love was swirling. It wrapped itself tightly around this new family of

I Told You Not To Climb The Cactus

three.

"I love you," I whispered to Ian when the doctor and the midwife were not looking.

Mum and the veteran mother were right. Your own kids are entirely different. This gorgeous baby did not look the least bit like a monkey. My maternal feelings had finally arrived and in the nick of time. I looked at my husband and smiled.

"She is the most beautiful baby in the world," he said.

I nodded in agreement.

"I wouldn't give you two cents for all the newborn babies in the hospital, but I would die for this one," I said with conviction.

Wendy Hamilton

New Parents.

The ultrasound showed a single baby. Therefore, I expected to give birth to only one new being. I did not know a mother is simultaneously born with her first child. Or that the labor that produces a mother, lasts long after the physical pain has subsided.

Fathers are also born along with their first child. Unlike me, Ian did not get a dollop of hormones when Marie was born. This retarded the process somewhat. He had taken the week off work to look after me. As I don't like hospitals and was in excellent health, I went home two hours after Marie was born. In preparation for the event, we had splurged and bought a microwave. Moreover, I had stocked the freezer with meals for a month. The system was working well for Ian. The microwave was going again (the third time before lunch) and tasty smells wafted through the air. The baby also was feeding. I lay in bed looking at her red-brown hair and tiny wrinkled fingers. It felt rough to be the only one in the house not eating.

I Told You Not To Climb The Cactus

"Hello," I shouted. "Do you think you could make some for me this time? I haven't had anything to eat since the hospital meal and I am very hungry."

"Sorry, I forgot about you." He bustled off to get another plate.

"I suppose this is why women usually get their mothers to help," I thought sourly.

There was another round of buzzing noises, and the ting of the microwave bell. I guessed that Marie had finished feeding because she had fallen asleep. I wrapped her up in a crotched blanket and put her in the bassinet beside the bed. I could hear bustling about in the kitchen and presently Ian came in carrying a plate of chicken stew.

"Here you go," he said, sitting the plate on my knees.

"Thank you Darls," I replied. "Do you think I could have something to eat it with? It's a bit hot for fingers."

"Oh yeah, I forgot," he said rushing out.

He was back in a second with a knife and fork. "I think I will go outside after lunch," he said as I started eating.

"Good idea," I encouraged. I was busting to go to the bathroom, but I did not want to go while he was around. I could not let him see me walking. That is just the silly sort of behavior that ensures a woman gets all her jobs back. Why do men think a woman on her feet means back to business as usual? I wondered as I ate chicken stew. I waited until I heard the backdoor slam before I crawled out of bed. I felt as light as a fairy now that the huge bowling ball of weight was removed from my front. Something weird had happened to my stomach muscles, however; they seemed to be missing, with the result that it was difficult to stand up straight. I shuffled out of the bedroom like a bent old woman. Unfortunately, I had to pass through the kitchen on

Wendy Hamilton

my pilgrimage to the bathroom. Dirty dishes were stacked like skyscrapers on the sink bench, cupboard doors hung open and the floor needed a good sweep. I averted my eyes and crept onwards. Business in the bathroom shortly after giving birth is not pleasant. I winced through the process and shuffled back to bed.

As I snuggled into the blankets hoping to catch up on much-needed sleep, a ladder reared up outside my window; the top of which slammed down on the guttering. Ian's legs, moving like pistons, stomped up the rungs. The feet stopped at the middle of the windowpane just before leaves and debris showered down. I sighed. This was going to be harder than I thought. Ian was very willing to help, but he did not think like a woman. I would much prefer he washed the dishes to cleaning the gutters. For the second time I wondered if I should have asked my mother to help. The scrabbling noises in the eves of the roof continued all afternoon; fading away as the ladder moved methodically around the perimeter of the house. I drifted off to sleep, only to be woken by the thin wailing of a newborn. Marie needed another feed. I lifted her out of the bassinet and juggled about clumsily. I was still new to this breastfeeding thing, but as the baby and I had the same idea in mind, we got it sorted out. Such a blessing to have no audience, I thought. I could feel the hunger rising in myself as Marie sucked contentedly. Surely it was dinnertime.

There was a metallic rattling and the sound of a big commotion in the basement directly below me. I guessed correctly that it was my husband putting away the ladder. Oh good, I thought, he must have finished. I expect he will be in soon. Sure enough, the backdoor squeaked open and Ian stumped in. I heard the soft bang of the freezer door and the

I Told You Not To Climb The Cactus

buzz of the microwave.

"Don't forget me this time," I bawled out.

"Yeah, yeah," Ian yelled, pretending he had remembered.

I was not fooled. The pause in the buzzing and the second bang of the freezer door told me all. A few minutes after the small *ting*, Ian arrived carrying two plates. Once again, I wrapped Marie firmly in the crotched blanket. Was she supposed to be lying on her left or her right side this time? I could not remember. Think, think, think Wendy. Was she facing me or the wall when I picked her up? A dim memory of her facing me surfaced through the fog. I was only one day into this and already I was sleep deprived. I lay her down facing the wall.

"Here you go," said Ian passing me a plate of beef stew. He plunked himself down in the chair that stood beside the bed and started eating. "I got all the gutters cleaned this afternoon and tomorrow I will stack the firewood properly and water-blast the path."

"I will need you to get some groceries tomorrow," I reminded him. "The fruit is getting low and we need toilet paper and tea bags."

"I'll have time for everything," said Ian breezily. He scraped the last of his stew off his plate with a piece of bread and munched it down.

The baby stirred, and a horrible smell permeated the room.

"Oh dear," I moaned as the thin wail started up. "I've only just started my dinner."

"Don't worry Wend, I'll deal with it," said Ian smacking his plate on the bedside table and leaping up. He bustled over to the cradle and whisked Marie out; jiggling her while he made bubbling noises. It was not the way I would have done it, but it worked a treat. Marie shut up and looked at him as he laid her on the end of the bed and unbuttoned her stretch-and-grow suit. It flopped baggily around her thin little bandy legs. "Where are the nappies?" he barked, stopping the bubbling noises momentarily.

"Under the bassinet," I replied. "You'll need the baby wipes and the barrier cream," I added as he rummaged boisterously under the long white drapery.

"Dere oo go, dat ill make oo feel better," cooed Ian cleaning the small bottom as if it were an engine that needed de-greasing. "Which way do these nappies go?" he asked pulling a disposable diaper out of its bag.

"The bunnies on the strip go to the front," I said confidently. I was the expert on diaper changing in this house because I had done it five times already. He gathered the ridiculously small ankles together in one hand and hoisted them aloft as he slid the diaper under her. The sticky tapes that held them in place gave him trouble and the end result looked somewhat lopsided, but that did not matter in the least.

"No, no, lie her facing the wall," I intervened as he put her back in the bassinet. "We don't want her head getting misshapen or worse still, pressure sores."

"OK," he said flipping her over.

A fussing sound, rising in intensity arose from the cradle.

"I forgot to burp her," I said horrified.

"I'll do it," said Ian, picking the baby up again. He slung her over his shoulder and patted her back. There was a large burp as Marie spat milk onto his shirt. Ian smiled and puffed out his chest. "That was a really good one," he said proudly.

"Yes, it was," I agreed, "you're good at burping. You're better at it than me, I think it must be your wider shoulders."

I Told You Not To Climb The Cactus

He did not reply but a smirk hovered at either end of his smile. He laid Marie down again. She was not pleased and showed it with small fussy noises.

"I hope the night won't be too bad," I said, putting my now empty plate on the bedside table. I leaned over and jiggled the side of the bassinet and the fussing noises stopped.

"How bad can it be?" said Ian naively

The answer was, pretty bad. The next morning, I had bags under my eyes. Ian, however, leaped out of bed, fully refreshed.

"What a good baby," he smiled, "she slept all the way through the night."

"Seriously, what planet are you on?" I asked him sourly, thinking the life of a man looked very attractive. "I had to feed and change her six times." The small being beside me, woke up and started to wail, "and she still wants more."

"You'll feel better after you've had something to eat. You feed her while I make breakfast," said Ian bustling out hastily.

There was a sound of crockery clattering and the smell of burning. Shortly after, he arrived with a plate of marmalade on toast.

"I'm sorry they are a bit black," he said sheepishly.

"I don't care," I said, shifting the baby so that one hand was free. I picked up a piece of toast heroically. "What I want more than anything is a nice cup of tea."

"We have a little problem with that," said Ian.

"What do you mean a problem?" I asked jerking my head up.

"We've run out of tea bags."

"No tea!" Suddenly I felt very emotional. "Well just

make me tea without the tea," I said pulling myself together with difficulty.

Ian cleared his throat uncomfortably. "We have run out of milk too. How about a cup of hot water?"

"It will have to do," I sniffed. Self-pity was knocking at my door. I hid my tears by putting the baby back into her crib. I should have got my mother to help, I thought, she would have remembered milk and tea bags.

Ian was not deceived by my ruse. "I'll go and get some now," he said, hurriedly rushing out.

I waited until I heard the car leave the driveway before getting out of bed and shuffling off to the bathroom. The risk of him thinking that I would be up to light duties escalated as the days passed.

He was away for a long time.

He must be doing a big buy up I thought, leaning back on my pillow after the bathroom ordeal. I remembered the skimpy little flap of tissue hanging next to the toilet and hoped he remembered toilet paper. Eventually, I heard the sound of the car pulling into the driveway and a great clattering as he leaped up the steep concrete steps at the back of the house. The back door squeaked open, slammed shut, and the all-providing-male bounced in like Tigger. He was waving a book.

"Look what I found," he crowed.

"A book!" I said in a tone like Eeyore. "I was hoping for tea bags not a book."

"Not just a book, it's *The New Testament Survey*! I have wanted one of these for ages."

"Where are the groceries, did you get any, or did you spend all your time in the Christian bookshop?" I asked morosely.

I Told You Not To Climb The Cactus

"Don't worry, I got them," he said breezily. The shopping trip had put him on a high. He rushed out and staggered back clutching a huge pile of disposable diapers. He dumped the packs on the end of the bed higgledy-piggledy. They looked like an avalanche of graffitied icebergs.

"What about the toilet paper, tea bags and all the other stuff I told you we needed?"

He reluctantly tore his attention away from the pages of his prize.

"Oh, he said a little shamefaced, I forgot about those."

Now I knew I should have asked my mother to come.

At least the loaded bed was evidence that the father part of his brain had been activated. The tunnel vision and sheer volume of his hunting-gathering expedition showed something deep and primeval had registered FATHERHOOD.

"I'll go again," he said absentmindedly as he perused his book.

"Get a pen and paper," I said, lunging at him and snatching his book away. "This time you will take a shopping list."

He shuffled off and returned with a notepad and pen.

"Write this in big letters," I said firmly, "Tea bags and milk."

"Yeah, yeah, whatever," he replied, as if my lack of trust was neurotic.

I glared at him and carried on dictating from a horizontal position. I spoke rapidly because the need to get up was escalating. Eventually he finished and went. I crawled out of bed and headed for the bathroom. On the way back I stopped for a drink of water. Oh, for a cup of tea, I thought crawling into bed. I hope he doesn't lose the list. I dropped off to sleep. The squeak of the back door awoke me. At last Ian was home and this time things were much better. He had forgotten nothing and I had my cup of tea. Even the dishes were getting done. I could hear clinks as he scrubbed plates energetically.

Somehow, we muddled through that first week. By the time the midwife called to check up on me, we were getting the hang of it.

"You seem very confident with babies," said Linley, watching me sling Marie around as I changed her, "have you had a lot of experience?"

"No, I have had no experience, only fat cats. They feel pretty much the same as a baby. I've been dressing up cats and carting them around since childhood."

I handed the baby to Ian who was deep in his New Testament Survey. He threw her over his shoulder and there was a big burp.

"And Ian has had dogs. Burping is similar to patting a mutt. I guess (like most people) the parenting skills must have been in us, it just took the emergency of a baby to bring them out."

I looked around. Despite the messy floor, dishes in the sink, and nearly starving, I was glad I had not had my mother take over. If Mum had been there, or I had stupidly got on my feet, things would have been different. As it was, right from the start Ian took over, confidently wading knee-deep into the sea of fatherhood. My husband would never think like a woman, but he was rapidly growing into a highly involved good dad, which was far better.

I Told You Not To Climb The Cactus

The Wounded Ego.

It is a fact of nature that kids dent a mother's ego. In considering the unpleasant effect of children on self-esteem, let us gloss over the huge range of indignities suffered in producing the small offender and zip straight to the first ego puncture. There he lies the crowning achievement of your life. For the last nine months you have scrimped and saved, painted and sewed (or at least shopped till your feet dropped) to produce a lovely designer nursery. (We are talking the ideal here not necessarily the truth.)

There is a draped crib, a shabby chic dresser with cabriole legs, and a rocking chair with a Rabbit stenciled on the seat. There is also a stack of baby clothes tenderly folded in the dresser. And whether your taste is Edwardian Christening gowns or stretchy black and yellow bumblebee suits, one thing is for sure. You picked the Silver Cross Nanny Pram or the Mountain Buggy as a foil to show off your prize.

But what does your little Lord Fauntleroy or cute wee bumblebee, do on the first public viewing? He gets acne.

Wendy Hamilton

I could feel the first pricks in my ego as I looked at Marie.

"What's happened to her?" I asked Linley as I peered at the pimples spreading over my baby's yellow skin.

"She's just a wee bit jaundiced, it's quite common," replied Linley unconcerned.

"What about all that," I said, pointing at the red bloom covering Marie's face. It rivaled the acne of the teenage boy-next-door (without the help of chips, coke and chocolate.)

"Her hormones are adjusting," explained Linley. "They are all over the place at the moment."

Marie's hormones were not the only ones all over the place. While my face resisted the temptation to make us a matching pair, my heart was not as immune. My emotions were as lumpy as a page of brail and not half so coherent.

"She looks fine," said Linley. She wrote 'normal' in Marie's baby book before giving it back to me. "This is my last visit, next check-up will be with the Plunket nurse," she reminded me.

"I remember. Thank you for all you have done, Linley," I said walking with her to the door.

"I'll see you next baby," she grinned.

"Hopefully that won't be in the near future," I smiled weakly as I walked with her to the door.

She had not been gone long when a steady stream of visitors hit the house. I had delayed the onslaught by refusing to stay in hospital. The hoard of well-wishers could not be held off forever, unfortunately.

"Oh, what a beautiful baby," they lied politely as I showed her off. The red bloom had flowered into small pus-filled blossoms. Furthermore, her curly hair (quite an achievement for a baby) now looked very motley. Patches of it had rubbed off at the back and around the sides. A nasty

I Told You Not To Climb The Cactus

smell wafted into the room and the visitors hastily departed.

I investigated Marie's under region cautiously.

Oh dear. There is no newborn diaper in the world that can stop yellow poop squirting out the leg holes I thought, surveying the damage. Poop had seeped through two layers of stretch-n-grows, down into her booties and onto the fine woolen shawl my grandmother had knitted for me when I was a baby.

A far greater effort, however, eclipsed even this accomplishment. What appeared to be thick acrylic paint had shot out of the top of her diaper, washed past her shoulder blades and finally stopped at the shoreline of her neck; the last wave dyed her downy hair duckling yellow.

Could I use this stuff to paint an adobe house? I wondered, curiously poking at it with a baby wipe. I was tempted to try. Pity I only had a weatherboard house. I started wiping the small bottom but quickly realized the normal clean-up-routine would not work for this Magnus Opus poop. I filled the baby-bath and stripped Marie gingerly, wiping away the excess yuck as best as I could. Although it was not pleasant, it was not anywhere as offensive as normal pooh. Another advantage of breastfeeding, I thought as I lowered her into the warm water. Marie waved her little arms and smiled at me. At this age (technically speaking) it was a wind grimace. I, however, like all mothers, knew it was a real smile. I smiled and babbled as I washed her. It took a while but eventually my baby was sweet-smelling again. By the time I had cleaned up the bathroom and dumped the dirty clothes in a bucket of water to soak, I felt exhausted. I made myself a cup of tea and a bite to eat. As soon as Marie heard the clink of crockery, she started fussing.

Just peachy, I thought sourly. Every time I want to eat,

she wants to eat first. I grabbed a large dinner plate and sat my cup and four sandwiches on it. I had not been a mother long, but already I was getting adept at multitasking. I picked up the plate with one hand and scooped my howling daughter up with the other, before trailing into the lounge and plunking myself into an armchair. I set my plate on a small table beside the chair and unbuttoned my blouse. The siren stopped as Marie started feeding. Oh bliss, she's shut up, I thought, munching sandwiches above her. I sipped my tea very carefully making sure not to spill any on her. Unfortunately, the thoughtfulness was not reciprocated. Right at the end, when she was fully tanked up, Marie threw up. It was another Magnus Opus, only this time it was from the top end. Milk and saliva cascaded down my front and into my jeans. Now it was my time for a bath; not a bad thing because the weather was hot and it did not take much to make me smell like a cheese factory. Nevertheless, it was another job on the seemingly endless round of work connected with a newborn. Moreover, there was no time for a leisurely soak with bath-salts and candles. The human siren on the other side of the wall ruined that idea. It must be that big plate of peas and cabbage I had last night, I thought ruefully. I forgot they give babies wind. I dried myself off and dressed in clean clothes. I wanted to have an afternoon sleep but there would be no rest with that racket going on.

"Let's go for a nice walkie," I said to my screaming infant. I picked her up, put her in the pram and slung my still pristine baby bag over the handles.

It was a short walk to a group of shops that straggled along the main road. The rumbling movement lulled Marie to sleep as I plodded along putting one foot in front of the other, struggling to stay awake myself.

I Told You Not To Climb The Cactus

As I neared a popular café, I saw an elegant woman standing by the crowded tables that spread onto the footpath. Beside the woman was a toddler. I could hear the toddler long before I saw the tonsils of his wide-open mouth. His howling drew all the eyes to his flustered mother. I cringed for her as she picked him up. Unbeknown to her, he was clutching the hem of her full skirt; and as he rose higher, her skirt ascended to mortifying regions.

She will be horrified when she realizes, I thought, cringing inwardly for her. The fact she was so neat and modestly dressed made the public exposure of her undergarments so much worse. I scooted past, aware that the toddler's loud crisis preceded his mother's silent one. While I was still contemplating the poor woman's embarrassment, I spied a figure in the distance flanked by two smaller figures. It was Dianne; a High School peer. The nasty and familiar feeling of inferiority, arose at the sight of her.

I looked down at my yellow pimply monkey in the pram.

I don't feel up to Dianne scoring off me today, I thought shuddering. Memories of her leaning over my shoulder pointing out my numerous spelling mistakes, surfaced unpleasantly. Spelling was not the only point of inferiority. Dianne came from a wealthy family and always had the right clothes. My clothes, however, never fitted in. Moreover, they looked particularly tatty next to Dianne's outfits. When it was fashionable to wear slave sandals that crossed behind your heel, mine crossed in front of the ankle. When ponchos were in, mine had two points not four like everyone else's. Even my school uniforms were not quite right. Mine had the small squares and the coarse calico of the old style, while my classmates had the big checks and polished cotton of the new style. Dianne and I lost touch once we left school

Wendy Hamilton

and I did not feel like renewing the acquaintance; especially today. I swung around abruptly and headed for home.

Two days later, however, I saw her again. Ian had kindly finished work early so I could have a small break. As I walked into the bank, I saw Dianne. She was looking very harassed in grubby old jeans and a wrinkled sweater. The two figures I had seen beside her in the distance, morphed at close range into two messy preschoolers. As I breezed in alone, with all the occupational filth recently removed from my person, she spotted me from the corner of her eye. She pretended she hadn't seen me but I knew she had because of the frenzy of pulling up pants, tucking in tops and smoothing down hair she suddenly subjected her children too.

I looked the other way mercifully.

I had seen all I needed to know.

All the hits my ego had suffered at school were avenged.

Two minutes with two preschoolers was all it took to level her to the dust.

I floated home with a new measure of confidence.

On very rare occasions, a kid's natural ability to shred a mother's ego will work in your favor!

Madonna and Child.

Although Mother Mary is an eternal muse for artists, I do not have a single print of that lovely woman hanging on my wall. It would be too depressing.

I have instead, a highly prized picture of a new mother and child. It sits in a tatty cardboard box shoved in the back of the closet. The box stores the family photos I am planning to make into beautiful albums the day I get sentimental and bedridden. I doubt this particular photo will make it into my albums, however, as both my girls vie for ownership.

There I sit, a young me propped up in bed. Hannah, a newborn baby, slumbers peacefully in my arms, while Marie beside me screams and I glare at her. The toddler's scream is silent but potent. There is aggression in every facial line and passion in the red crumpled complexion. It is not the expression of a good, sinless child. The mother's glare is also silent but speaks equal volumes. It is not the gentle, loving look of a blue-robed Madonna. It is not a profile picture you would want to put on social media to announce your new arrival.

It does, however, capture perfectly my dual emotions; of nurture towards the newborn and flashes of hostility to the former baby.

"How did this bottom get so large and why isn't it potty trained?" I fussed to Ian as I changed Marie's diaper.

"Beats me," said Ian putting away his camera (he had just captured the prized picture.)

"You've got the better job," I said wiping the big bottom. "Compared to a toddler, cleaning a new baby is pleasant."

To make things even worse, both kids were bawling. The thin wailing coming from his side of the room was much easier to cope with, however, than the foghorn bellowing below me. That hideous sound shattered my day far too frequently. I finished my task and stood Marie on the ground. She immediately lifted up her arms.

"No, you don't need me to carry you around," I said looking at her big sturdy legs. "You're a big girl now you can walk places by yourself."

The foghorn bawling increased. To stop the dreadful noise, I picked her up and sat her on my hip resentfully. She switched off the racket and stuck her thumb in her mouth. I left the room and wandered out to the kitchen. The dishes needed washing and the laundry was piling up. I put Marie down on her strong legs and looked at her speculatively as Ian came in.

"I think Marie is big enough to help a bit," I said firmly. "What is it about the second child that quadruples the work?"

"I dunno," said Ian scratching his head. "Mathematically speaking, it is only twice the work."

I Told You Not To Climb The Cactus

The second baby.

Wendy Hamilton

"One-plus-one-equals-two completely collapses if each one is a *little one,*" I snorted, as I stopped Marie from eating the cat's biscuits. "I think it is because numbers don't come with legs.

"Putting two in the car triples the work," agreed Ian.

"Absolutely," I said vehemently.

Ian looked thoughtful. "It would help if you could hang Marie off the side vision mirror while you put the baby in," he said at last.

I wished his idea was feasible. I thought of it wistfully as I buckled Hannah into her car seat the next day. What a pity toddler's overalls did not come equipped with a grappling hook. Unfortunately, I had to grow rear mirrors myself as my task was frequently interrupted by dashes into the traffic.

"No Marie, get back here!" I yanked her away from an oncoming truck. "We don't play on the road." The truck was still some distance away, but it felt like I had rescued her in the nick of time. My adrenaline was pumping and my legs felt weak. I had no idea I could sprint that fast.

"I want you to stay beside me," I pointed to a spot on the footpath.

A wail rent the air. Hannah had managed to drop her pacifier down the crack between the seats and the ring of giant keys into the gutter.

I retrieved the keys but was too distracted, however, to notice the loss of the pacifier.

Unfortunately, the baby was not so absent-minded. She escalated into howling. I realized my oversight as soon as I looked for something to stop the noise.

"Oh, dear, where is it?" I muttered, as I searched for it frantically. Meanwhile, Hannah was getting more and more wound up. The confined space of the car magnified

I Told You Not To Climb The Cactus

the wailing into a siren. Now I was just as wound up as Hannah without the option of tears, however. Eventually I discovered that I had buckled Marie's booster-seat over top of the pacifier. I retrieved it (with difficulty) and plugged the noise hole. Mercifully the siren stopped.

By the time I got Marie strapped into the car, my temper was frayed.

That was when I discovered she had taken off her shoes. Now she was not the only one who had lost something.

When I got my temper under control, I retrieved the missing shoes and shoved them back on her feet; not tenderly, however.

This time it was her turn to yell.

The pacifier fell out of the baby's mouth and the siren started up again.

I glanced at my watch as I slid behind the steering wheel.

"Please Lord," I prayed, "I need green lights all the way and may the doctor not be on time."

As I drove, the kids (lulled by the movement) went quiet. The wheels of the car spun me a small window of reprieve. I was painfully aware, however, that I was embroiled in an inevitable chain of events. I pulled into the doctor's car park and my reprieve ended as the chain of inevitability started up again. The next few minutes were torn into fragmented snippets.

I parked the car and reversed the car seat ordeal. Then repeated it on a magnified scale with the stroller.

"*Stand here Marie while I get Hannah out.*" (I pointed to a spot beside me.)

"*Come back Marie, wait here.*" (A worn-out phrase. As usual I had to say it more than once.)

Of course, there was a problem with the ticket vending

machine.

"*I said hold on to the side of the pushchair.*" (Another overworked sentence.)

I picked up the pacifier ten times, (three seconds on the ground equals still clean.)

"*No, you can't have that old chewing gum on the pavement Marie!*" (Thank goodness for eyes in the back of my head.)

Finally, the machine spat out a ticket. I grabbed it, rushed over to the car and bunged it on the dashboard.

Unfortunately, it was easy to lose small car keys in a large handbag.

At last the car was locked. (All was not well, however.)

"*Naughty girl, spit it out!*" (I frantically dug the filthy blob out of Marie's mouth.)

I glanced at my watch anxiously as I bounced the stroller up the doctor's concrete steps. (Pity help those in wheelchairs.)

"*Do worms have teeth?*"

"*I don't know. You'll have to ask Daddy tonight.*"

I disentangled the stroller from the high-pressure door.

Finally, the chain ended as I slumped into the doctor's waiting room.

"Hello, Wendy, how are you?" the receptionist greeted me.

"Good, fine," I told the big lie slickly as I sat down close to the toy section.

"Give the truck back Marie, we don't snatch," I admonished my daughter.

"I'm so sorry," (To the mother.)

Ominous snuffling coming from my stroller, caused me to jiggle it hastily.

I Told You Not To Climb The Cactus

Marie brought me a book. I lifted her on to my knee and read her thirty-four pages of Woofie the Wonder Dog. It should have been thirty-five pages but the last page was missing.

"What happened to Woofie, did the big dog eat him?" Marie wanted to know.

"Mrs. Hamilton," the nurse calling my name saved me the job of making up an ending to the story.

I got the baby out of the stroller and corralled everyone into a side room. The nurse weighed Hannah and took my blood pressure efficiently.

"Hmmm, that's strange," she said looking slightly concerned. "Your blood pressure is higher than usual."

She was an older woman. It was apparent from her next words that she suffered from amnesia; she had forgotten what parenting small children was like. She smiled at my brood like a blue-robed Madonna and said serenely, "just enjoy them, they are gone so fast."

Fat chance of that!

I did not need a fancy piece of equipment to know that my blood pressure had spiked at her words. I could feel it throbbing through my veins.

The woman was unrealistic, but so was I. Her comment hung in my head throughout the homeward trial and penciled itself into two ugly words, GUILT and FAILURE. I filed them into a tatty box in the back closet of my mind.

"I know my children are a blessing from God, but I just can't see it," I admitted shamefaced to a friend, as I recuperated from my ordeal.

"Wendy, now is not the time to look for blessings," she answered wisely.

She was right. Training small children is like laying

Wendy Hamilton

foundations. Digging trenches in the blistering sun is hard work. It is insensitive to say to a woman with a heavy pickaxe, "just enjoy the experience it will be over so quickly." While kids have their cute side, is more realistic to regard lovely moments as small oases in a big desert.

If (like me) you often fail to enjoy the experience of rearing small children, do not add guilt to your own tatty box. There is a place for just gritting your teeth and getting the job done. It is only after a house is built that you enjoy its shelter.

I Told You Not To Climb The Cactus

Socialization.

Baby Hannah lay in a cloth hammock that hung from fishing scales. She looked like a baby in a sling on an *It's-a-Girl* greeting card. The elderly unmarried Plunket nurse, however, did not look like a stork; she looked more like a stout sergeant major.

"I haven't seen you at the playgroup yet. We run it every Tuesday," she said sternly as she filled *'normal'* in all the little boxes of Hannah's Plunket book.

"No" I mumbled. I was glad I had my hands full with re-dressing my howling baby and did not have to look at her. Hannah had not appreciated shedding all her clothes on a winter morning for the routine checkup. Two-year-old Marie stood pulling at my skirt and whined to go home. I braced myself for the next part of the nurse's speech. I knew from experience, what was coming.

"Small children need socialization," she boomed in a voice rich with authority.

I thought about playgroups and shuddered. While some

Wendy Hamilton

women enjoyed them, I did not. We had this talk every check-up, but I had no intention of buckling. Dealing with my own kids was bad enough. I had enough experience in the church crèche to put me off forever, without adding a Plunket playgroup to it. Although I am not a fortune teller, I had no trouble visualizing myself at one of those ghastly events. I see myself in my mind's eye smiling with a sickly insincere grin at the mother of a small boy. Her three-foot-delinquent has just hit my child hard with a wooden bus.

"Don't worry about it, kids will be kids you have a lovely little boy," I lie through gritted teeth as I push myself between the small Hitler and my bawling toddler. While I am still talking, there is a scuffle behind me and a crisis erupts close to my back. I turn in time to see Marie snatching a toy from another child.

"Give Santa Bear back Marie," I admonish her, "we don't snatch other people's toys! I am so sorry" (to the mother). She smiles at Marie with a sickly insincere grin.

"Don't worry about it, kids will be kids you have a lovely little girl." The social lie slips out easily.

I wrestle the bear from my daughter's unyielding hands and return the toy to her howling victim.

"Here, play with Mr. Bobo instead, nice Mr. Bobo," I try in vain to distract her with another toy.

"Don't want Mr. Bobo, want Santa Bear."

"Well you can't have Santa Bear you need to share. Why don't you play tea parties with Jennifer over there?"

"Don't wanna play with that girl. I wanna go home."

I look around at all the preschool children. Not one child is playing with another (if you don't count fighting and snatching as legitimate social interactions). There are a couple of three-year-olds that fake it. They sit side by

I Told You Not To Climb The Cactus

side lost in their own separate worlds, playing their own individual game. They are twins. They put up with the chaotic environment but they would prefer the familiar atmosphere of home

A four-year-old erupts into a screaming tantrum as his mother attempts to prize a purple crayon out of his mouth.

"So sorry," she apologizes to the woman trying to pacify the child with the half colored in purple duck.

"Don't worry, (Purple-Duck's mother is gracious) kids will be kids, you have a lovely little boy, my kids eat crayons all the time."

All this tiny-tot 'socialization,' is having a strange unraveling effect on my maturity level. I feel it sinking to the lowest common denominator and suddenly I want to burst into tears like a two-year-old. Like my child, I wanna go home too.

"So, I expect to see you all next Tuesday?" the nurse's voice pulls me back into reality. I look at her and wonder if she has ever sat for hours and observed what really goes on between small children when they interact. She is elderly, single and has never been a mother. I seriously doubt she has ever spent large quantities of time with small children. Probably she bases all her authority on textbooks written by experts who have never raised children.

Like cabbage patch babies and the stork who brings them, the idea that small kids need socialization is a myth.

"No, I don't think so," I say firmly as I buckle Hannah into the stroller.

"Come on Marie it is time to go home."

Wendy Hamilton

Guerilla Warfare.

She talked like Winston Churchill and was born to rule the world. I was the pinnacle of her world so that meant conquering me.

I thought about my preschooler with mounting dislike. I could hear her high-pitched words shooting at me as she came down the hallway. For her age her vocabulary was impressive. It is possible, however, to overdo anything and I was worn out by the incessant onslaught. The only time Marie ever stopped talking was when she was asleep. Even left alone in her bedroom for an afternoon quiet time, the mouth kept up its steady machine-gun rattle. I could hear the shrill little voice as she played with her toys.

"Now Jane, it's time to go to the hospital to get your head sewn back on. Get in the car…….Brrrrrrrrm, la, la, la, la, la…..hello nurse, Jane has had an accident you have to sew her head back on. Oh no doctor, you have put it on the wrong way. That's better, lie there quietly Jane while the nurse takes your temperature….. Now you have to have a

I Told You Not To Climb The Cactus

Cat-scan like Grandma…..weeeeeee….."

I looked at the clock and sighed. Two fifty; ten more minutes before the alarm clock released her back into my world. I sucked up the last few minutes like a man in the desert drinks his last cup of water.

Bizzzzzz.

There was a thump and Jane received another head injury as she fell unheeded to the floor. A quick staccato of running feet and suddenly my peace was breached. Poor Jane, neither she nor any of the other toys could compete with the game of Conquer-the-Mother. I was far more exciting. Like Jane, I also lost my head but in a much noisier and reactive way. The skirmishes between us added zest to Marie's life.

"Can I have a biscuit, what are you doing, when is Daddy coming home, why do trees grow up, why is it dark at night?" Her questions rained down on me.

"You can have a biscuit after you have helped me tidy up your room," I said honing in on one question. I walked down the hallway and she trailed behind me. The room as I expected was a mess.

"Pick up Jane and put her away," I said opening the toy box. "And all the soft toys go in here too."

I started gathering up the crayons scattered about the floor. Sniff, sniff, I paused and sniffed the air. There was a foul smell. Instantly I was on alert. Potty training was not going too well and I was not in the smug group of mothers who could boast that their child was toilet trained before two.

"Do you need your nappy changed?"

"Noooo," She looked at me with hooded eyes and a smile I did not like.

"Are you sure?" I caught her as she meandered past me

dragging a teddy bear by his ear.

"Yes."

Something in the tone of her voice added the smell of a rat to the stink in the room.

I lifted her up and smelled her lower regions. Surprisingly, that was not where the pong was coming from. I put her down and went about the room sniffing like a bloodhound. It seemed to be coming from the small table under the window. Sniff, sniff. No, there was nothing under the table and the long curtains smelled alright. Sniff, sniff. It was coming from the coloring book on the table. I opened it up. A lion covered in green scribbles stared back at me sadly. A small pooh the size and texture of a sheep dropping was squashed onto the top of his head.

"Marie, did you do this?" I asked, looking at her with thin lips and hard eyes.

"No," she lied glibly. "The lion did it."

"The lion did not do it," I said emphatically.

"Yes, he did," she was equally emphatic. The hooded look over her eyes narrowed into slits.

I turned the page. "What about these," I said pointing to several more poohs.

"The horse and the penguin did them." Her eyes slid about as she scanned the floor.

"Look at me young lady," I demanded, "and stop telling such big lies."

Marie stared at me unrepentantly, a tricky little look on her face. I did not like the tricky little look. I could not put my finger on what was wrong with it, but it made my blood boil.

I investigated the rest of the book in increasing horror. On almost every page I found a small pooh.

I Told You Not To Climb The Cactus

"Can I have a biscuit now?" The question was demanding and the look brazen. The heat in my blood went up another degree. I was about to answer when something poking out from under the bed caught my eye. I lifted the valance and saw an empty diaper. I grabbed her hands and inspected them closely.

"Absolutely not!" I shouted losing my head. "This is disgusting behavior!"

I marched her off to the bathroom and scrubbed her hands with soap and disinfectant. She watched me with a calculating pout on her face. As I dumped the pillaged diaper and soiled book into the trash, my small opponent shifted gears and changed tactics.

The baby started howling.

"Marie, come here please, I want you in the lounge where I can keep an eye on you." It was a command and she came alright, one inch at a time, with agonizing slowness. It was not obedience nor outright defiance. I dithered, unsure how to react.

"Why do I have to come, Mum, huh why do I have to come? Does Fluffy Face have to come? Can I have a drink? Why does the cat have fluffy hair? I'm hungrrrry." She shuffled forward little by little.

I was a beginner-mother pitted against a professional-kid. She was born fully wired while my programming system was still in the construction mode. At least my alarm was up and running. It sounded out loud and clear in red waves of anger. Unfortunately, the correct response was still packed in its box. I should have asked myself, "what is the naughty little hound doing………. what have I missed?"

Instead, I eyed her with dislike and asked myself, "does she feel loved?" The question roasted me emotionally. Guilt heaped on top of anger. Dreadful mother, poor little insecure child, no child deserves a mother that can't stand them. These and similar thoughts bludgeoned me.

The baby increased her howling as it was time for her feed.

I remembered certain chapters in child psychology books. Perhaps Marie is getting very naughty because of jealousy towards the baby, I pondered as I picked up Hannah. I had noticed my firstborn vied for attention when I fed the baby. I Carried Hannah through to the lounge and sat down in my favorite armchair.

"You can play quietly with the blocks," I instructed Marie, pointing to a basket of blocks as I unbuttoned my top. The howling stopped magically as Hannah started feeding. We had not been into it more than two minutes when Marie interrupted me.

"I don't want to play with the blocks," she said, throwing one across the room.

I fixed her with a hard look and was about to give her a sound telling off when the thought 'jealousy' hit me. "Don't throw blocks, Marie. Go and get your dolly with the bottle and you can feed your baby," I said, swallowing down my annoyance with difficulty.

Marie trailed off into her bedroom and I continued feeding Hannah. A minute later she returned empty-handed. The tricky little look was back on her face, however.

"I can't find her."

"Did you look in the toy box?"

There were the hooded eyes again. "She wasn't there."

"What about under your bed?"

"She wasn't there either." The tone I distrusted was also back.

I Told You Not To Climb The Cactus

I hoisted myself out of the chair, trying to joggle Hannah as little as possible. Still feeding her, I walked through to Marie's room.

"There she is, lying right in the middle of the floor," I said in exasperation.

"Where?" asked Marie looking at the ceiling.

"Stop staring at the ceiling and open your eyes," I hissed, my temper rising. I stuffed it back down with increasing difficulty.

Marie picked up her doll by the leg and trailed behind me as I made my way back to the armchair. I eased myself down smoothly and used my free arm to pull the cushion into the small of my back.

"I don't know where the bottle is."

"Why didn't you say something when I was in there?" I fumed.

Marie smirked and shrugged her shoulders. Something about that smirk felt like fingernails down a chalkboard.

"Go and have another look for it."

She was back horribly fast. "It's not there."

"Go and have another look."

She went into her room and came straight back

"It's not there."

I hoisted myself out of the chair again. "There it is," I snapped, pointing to the missing article lying in full view on her bed.

She picked it up and once again I retraced my steps and eased myself back into the chair. For three minutes there was peace. I closed my eyes as exhaustion engulfed me. I was rudely awakened by the bottle hitting my head.

"Stop that Marie. That was very naughty. Go and stand in the naughty corner with your face to the wall," I barked.

Wendy Hamilton

Hannah threw up her hands in a startled reflex at the sound of my raised voice. "Hurry up," I hissed, stroking the downy head in the crook of my arm. My opponent shuffled slowly across the room. Once again it was not obedience, but neither was the behavior out-and-out defiance. My rage increased as did my feelings of guilt. Eventually, she got to the corner.

"Can I play now?" The tone that should have been subdued and submissive was loud and demanding.

"No, you have only been there one minute. I'll tell you when you can come out."

"I want a drink."

"No."

"I'm hungry I want a biscuit."

"I told you that you are not having one as a punishment, don't ask me for one again."

She twisted her head around cheekily and stared at me from the corner of her eyes. "Can't I have one ever and ever again?"

"Tomorrow you can. Turn around and face the wall."

"Here puss-puss."

"Be quiet and leave the cat alone." Why did I feel that eyes were rolling on the side of the head I could not see?

"Do birds have teeth?"

I ignored the question and all the ones that followed.

"I need to go potty."

That one got a direct hit. I lurched out of the chair in record speed and sprinted into the bathroom. Hannah (dislodged) sent up a wail. I grabbed the necessary equipment, rushed back into the lounge and plunked it on the floor beside my chair. "Hurry up and sit on the potty." I gripped her shoulder and compelled her towards it. I helped her onto the small throne and sat down again. Hannah stopped howling as she

I Told You Not To Climb The Cactus

started to feed once more.

"I'm finished," smirked Marie standing up.

"You haven't done anything," I said looking in the suspiciously empty potty. "Sit down and try again." I shut my eyes and tried to get a grip on the purple wave of frustration building up in me like steam in a pressure cooker.

"I can't do anything." There was that hideous expression on her face again.

The dislike grew into something akin to loathing. The waves of purple and red turned into gray guilt. What did the psychology book advocate? I wracked my brains. Ah, that's right.

"When I've finished feeding Hannah, I will read you a story and we can have a Mummy and Marie special time," I said with an insincere smile.

I could not have played into the little tyrant's hands better. The tricky look changed into smug arrogance.

It took a seasoned mother to rescue me. Mum came and gave me a much-needed break one morning. Oh, the bliss to wave them goodbye for two hours. When they got back, my mother had vital information for me.

"Wendy, that child of yours has got you on toast!" she said. (Mum's alarm system was honed with years of experience of me.) "She is doing naughty little things all the time."

The truth of my mother's words washed over me like a balm, and a huge sense of relief flooded me. It was as if my soul knew what was wrong and was craving validation. Somehow all the books on child-rearing and psychology had gagged and shut down my gut instinct. "When you were that age, I used to take you to see your Grandmother and she would say, how's my good little girl, you wouldn't smack my good little girl?" continued my mother. "Even at age two, you were smart enough to know that I wouldn't discipline you in front of your Grandmother. The minute we got to her door you would get a smirk on your face and become a proper little toad, naughty as can be."

"I know that look," I said bitterly, "I often see it on Marie's face."

"Well, this went on until I tumbled to it," continued my mother.

"What did you do?" I asked, I had a great memory, but it did not go back that far.

"The next time you were naughty and my mother-in-law said, you wouldn't smack my good little girl? I gave your chubby leg an unpleasant slap with my hand. Grandma, THIS is how we keep her a good little girl, I said."

"What did she say?" I asked.

"She just said, I suppose so. I never had another problem with you at Grandma's after that."

My relief turned into peace. Thank goodness for the sense of an older woman. One thing still nagged at me, however.

"I worry that Marie is insecure and jealous of the baby."

"Wendy, that child of yours just wants to know if you are still the boss and if the rules have changed now that there is a new baby."

I was grateful to my mother for her sage words.

I thought of James Dobson another voice of sanity. What was it he said? I tried to remember. That's right if you draw a line in the dirt and say don't come over this line and your two-year-old flops his big toe over it, he is looking for a fight, don't disappoint him, or words to that effect.

My daughter was looking for a fight and I was

I Told You Not To Climb The Cactus

disappointing her. The all-absorbing question in her little mind was, how strong are you? Are you powerful enough to be a worthy leader?

My mother and James Dobson had given me a vital tool for my motherhood arsenal. I did not have to wait long to try it out.

Bizzzzzz. Unfortunately, three o'clock had rolled around again. Two small feet pounded out of Marie's bedroom and catapulted into my space.

"I'm hungrrrrry, can I have a biscuit?"

I was about to answer the normal, "not until you have tidied your room," when something arrested my attention.

"Have you been into my lipstick Marie?"

"Nooo," the lie slipped out glibly from between huge clown lips. There was the tricky little smirk and the hooded eyes again.

"Don't lie to me," I said stomping into her room. A tube of lipstick (half-eaten) lay sprawled on the dressing table. Gashes of red slashed the mirror above it. "You've been very naughty," I steamed, pointing to the graffiti.

"It wasn't me, it was Jane." The hoods turned into slits as her eyes slid across the floor to the headless doll.

I remembered my mother's advice and acted on it. I gave Marie a stinging slap on the meaty part of her leg. Unexpectedly, peace and wellbeing filled my soul. All my anger and pent up steam evaporated.

When Marie stopped howling, I gave her a hug.

"I love you too much to let you tell lies and be naughty like that," I said.

"I love you too Mummy," she said hugging me back. I looked into her eyes and saw something that amazed me. They had pinged wide open. The horrible hooded eyelids and narrow slits had disappeared, as had the tricky look and nasty little smirk. My daughter had the wide-eyed look of innocent childhood once again.

I would like to be able to say everything from that point was good. We had many more skirmishes, however. I had to prove to my daughter beyond a shadow of a doubt I was a worthy leader.

While the smack has gone out of favor and is not politically correct in many countries, never underestimate its power of cleansing if you are dealing with blatant disobedience. A small child who continuously wins against his mother is not a happy or secure child. There are many methods to conquer the will without breaking the spirit. A well-timed smack is merely one tool. The bottom line is, a mother must fight hard in the early years to establish the right to lead.

I Told You Not To Climb The Cactus

A Bonding Moment.

My mother had some strange sayings. If an animal was particularly attractive, she called it a 'chocolate box' puppy or kitten or whatever. Back in her youth, a chocolate box was a work of art worth saving. They made pretty storage containers for odds and ends like ribbons, cotton reels, or recycled buttons. The glossy kittens or puppies on the lids were always immaculately clean, with melting innocent eyes. They sat adorably in baskets or played delightfully with tidy balls of wool. When Mum saw an unusually pretty baby sitting in a pram, she called it a chocolate-box-baby. Chocolate-box-baby was the ultimate compliment.

Well, right now I had a chocolate-box-baby, but I was feeling far from complimentary. She was sitting in the middle of the kitchen floor rug, surrounded by a battlefield of fallen Hazel Nut Crèmes, Strawberry Swirls, and Dairy Milk Delights. Her chubby cheeks puffed out tautly like two little red golf balls with a chocolaty hole between them. She was not clean and her eyes were not innocent. Furthermore, it was her bottom, not her face that sat on the lid of the box.

I shrieked.

"Ian the baby has got your birthday chocolates!"

There was a thundering sound as Ian's legs moved like pistons down the hallway. Chocolates were a luxury we seldom got.

"How did she get them off the table?" he yelled sliding to a halt beside the wreckage.

"I have no idea," I answered looking puzzled. "She's two-and-a-half foot high and not even walking yet."

"Did you leave them on the floor? asked Ian suspiciously.

"Of course not."

"How did she get them unaided and so quickly then?"

"I have no idea," I said mystified. "I don't even know how she knew there were chocolates in the box."

"Did Marie help her?"

"No, she has been with me all morning," I said blowing that theory to bits.

We surveyed the battlefield sadly. Most of the chocolates were wounded in some way, many missing bite-sized chunks. Even the foil-wrapped ones had deep lacerations; their silver and gold armor pierced by four deadly sharp teeth.

"I wish she had left the caramel centers alone," I wailed, looking at the sticky brown ooze on Hannah's face and hair.

"They have made a mess," said Ian handing me a damp cloth.

As I wiped my daughter's face, I noticed something from the corner of my eye. I paused and turned my head for a better look.

"I think some of the chocolates have rolled under the

I Told You Not To Climb The Cactus

oven," I said excitedly.

Ian kneeled down and squinted into the darkness. "Ooo, you're right." He slipped his hand under the crack and tried to hook them out with his fingers. "Blast them," he exploded as several chocolates rolled away into obscurity.

"Use the broom handle," I said handing him one out of the broom cupboard.

He snatched it and trawled the murky depths systematically.

"I wondered where those had got to," I said as a thimble and an egg-timer came to the light.

"And my good screwdriver," said Ian putting it in his pocket. "These look salvageable," he said picking up four chocolates. He blew the dust off them, popped one in his mouth, and plunked the others on the bench.

"You're a messy pup," I said to my chocolate-box-baby. She smiled at me and two half-sucked chocolate-almonds popped out of her mouth. They fell down her toweling stretch-n-grow, dragging brown trails of slobber behind them. I wiped the mess out of Hannah's hair as best I could before turning my attention to her hands. Melted chocolate squished out from between her fingers.

"The Vanilla Crème's are gonners," I said regretfully, as I prized a podgy hand open and inspected the damage.

"We might be able to save the fudge centered ones," said Ian optimistically. He had found some clustered by the fender.

"That's good."

"She has licked them but other than that they are alright." He gathered them up gingerly, washed them tenderly and set them on a cake rack to dry.

I walked over to the bench and peered at them.

Wendy Hamilton

A bonding moment

I Told You Not To Climb The Cactus

"I'm glad they have survived, they're my favorite."

I rinsed out my cloth and moved back towards Hannah who was still sitting on the lid of the chocolate box. In the middle of my journey, something squished under my foot. I stood on one leg and scraped the messy blobs off my slipper.

"Oh no, she has squashed Peppermint Creams into my floor rug," I howled in fury.

"Technically, you're the one who has squashed them into the rug," said Ian.

"*Not helping*," I hissed at him. I hated it when he got all nitpicky over details.

Meanwhile, Marie (attracted by the commotion) stood at the doorway chanting in a sing-song voice over and over,

"Bubby's been naughty, Bubby's been naughty!" Admiration was written all over her face. She went close to her little sister and patted her on her head. "Clever Bubby."

As a token of friendship and goodwill, Hannah handed Marie the mass graveyard of vanilla crèmes.

Marie took them with gratitude.

Unnoticed by Ian and I who were still scrubbing chocolates and the floor rug respectively, there was a tender bonding moment between the two little girls that gladdened the hearts of the demons sent up from below.

I finished dabbing the rug and put a few salvaged chocolates away in the fridge.

"You know," I said to Ian through gritted teeth, "people who go on about the terrible twos are a year too late in their calculations."

Wendy Hamilton

Telephone troubles.

All days have twenty-four hours, but not all days are equal. They usually show their colors early. Unfortunately, the ratio of good to bad is not an equal fifty-fifty; especially if you have small children. If you are a mother, the dark days can outnumber the light ones.

This morning, however, bode well. My energy level was up (hallelujah) the house was tidy and twenty-four little bread rolls sat in the oven, snuggly growing like puffballs in damp weather.

"Here you go," I said to Marie and Hannah as I plunked play-dough on their small table. It was fresh and still warm. In a burst of efficiency, I had whipped it together while I cooked breakfast. "Marie go and get the play-dough stuff out of the toy box and make something beautiful."

She rushed off obediently and returned clutching a container of plastic cookie cutters and rolling pins. Instant

I Told You Not To Climb The Cactus

obedience, a good omen.

Before long Miss. Four-year-old and Miss. Two-year-old were busy making elaborate creations. Moreover, they were not fighting, another good sign.

I poured myself a cup of tea and glided down the hallway and into the lounge where my telephone sat (like all the olden day phones) firmly tied to the wall.

I picked up the bulky receiver. Its coiled umbilical cord fell from my ear down to a chunky cream box with a round dial. I put my index finger into strategic holes and called my mother. Buzz, buzz….buzz, buzz. There was a small click as she picked her phone up.

"Hello?" "Hi Mum, I've got time to talk this morning."

"Hello, Dear, that's nice."

As my mother returned my greeting, I listened with half an ear to the reassuring prattle and industrious little thumps and bangs coming from the kitchen.

"You wouldn't believe what happened to me yesterday Mum. Remember the silly song you used to sing to us,

"My Mum said to me, don't put beans in your ears?"

"I haven't heard that one for years," laughed Mum.

"Well, I wish I had sung something like it to my kids about camellia buds up noses! We spent two hours at the doctors yesterday, all because Marie had the daft inspiration to ram one up her nostril."

"Oh dear! Tttt," tisked Mum.

"It was one heck of a job to get it out. I was on the phone when it happened of course."

"Of course." Mum's agreement was wholehearted.

"They get so naughty when I'm on the phone!"

"Kids always take advantage of a mother on the phone," Mum spoke matter-of-factly as if she was referring to a law of nature.

"That reminds me, hang on a minute Mum while I see what they are up to."

I put the receiver down, slipped quietly along the hallway and poked my head around the kitchen door. The day that had started so well, continued in goodness. Instead of two small children, I saw two little angels. On the table were lots of lumpy-cakey-things and two teacups. I sneaked back and picked up the receiver again.

"It's all right they are having a tea party." I sighed. "I wish they would invent phones you could carry around it would make life so much easier."

"I bought a long extension cord for mine the other day," said Mum. "It winds up like a hose reel. I'm sitting on the garden seat outside right now."

"Wow, I need one of those," I said thinking of the camelia bud and yesterday's wasted afternoon. "How long are they?"

"Twenty-foot-long!"

"Twenty-foot," I gasped "What a great idea."

"Annie's Emporium sells them."

"Good old Annie's. Trust it to be Annie's. I'll have a look at them next week when I go to town."

Now that the telephone troubles were fully explored, we moved on.

"The new neighbors have shifted in next-door," said Mum changing the subject.

"Have you met them yet?" I asked.

"Yes, and they are lovely. He's a nice little man and she knows Noleen and Max. They used to go to the little church in Wellington when we……"

Mum filled me in lengthily. When she had finally

I Told You Not To Climb The Cactus

finished, I hung up the phone. It had been a great talk… a long talk… an interesting talk…so interesting in fact, I had forgotten to keep one ear on the tea party.

The room down the hallway was suspiciously quiet. Time to investigate. I rounded the kitchen door and almost slipped on a large spreading puddle.

Someone had left the kitchen tap on.

Water, like a silver ribbon, fell into the overflowing sink before slipping down the front of the cupboards in a gentle waterfall. Every cupboard was open and pots lined the shelves.

The pots were filled to the brim with sudsy water while the shelves beneath them swam in slops. They were swollen and their usually flat surface was covered in corrugations. The morning's prediction of A Great Day took a serious credibility hit. I rushed over and turned off the running water.

"Girls where are you," I shouted through the red mist of rising anger. No answer.

I sloshed through the puddles, squelched over my poor floor rug and stomped out the back door. I found them sitting at the garden table under a large spreading tree.

"You girls have been very naughty, there is water everywhere," I yelled. The red mist was turning into purple rage. "You can come in right now and clean it up."

"We did the dishes and I made Hannah a yummy drink," Marie's cheery little voice piped up unrepentantly.

I turned my attention to the table and the hot anger changed instantly into cold terror. The angelic little tea party inside had morphed into a big deadly feast outside. Amidst the lumpy salt and flour cakes sat a carton of apple juice and several bottles of cleaning products.

"Hannah doesn't like it very much," Marie continued

unabashed.

Suddenly I noticed a large tumbler of unidentified liquid beside my toddler. The cold terror turned into ice that froze my blood into icicles.

The question, how did they get the kiddy-lock off the laundry cabinet? was eclipsed by a much bigger question. "How much has she drunk?" I croaked out.

It was hopeless trying to get that kind of information from a four-year-old. I thought about some of the bottles on the table. One, in particular, increased my terror. A child could be poisoned in twenty minutes by that stuff. I grabbed Hannah, forced a cup of milk down her throat and then frantically called a taxi.

"To the hospital," I barked as I bundled everyone in hastily.

It was late afternoon by the time I staggered through the front door of my home again. Early Morning was a false prophet.

Four hours in Accident and Emergency could not be called good by any stretch of the imagination. I was eternally thankful to God that it seemed unlikely that Hannah had taken much, if any, of Marie 'yummy' deadly cocktail. They both seemed perfectly normal and unlike me, still full of energy.

"Oh goody, our cakes are still there," said Marie skipping into the kitchen.

I looked at the messy table and remembered with horror my gently rising bread. I opened the oven. A gigantic spongy glob oozed out of the door and slid down onto the sodden un-mopped floor.

It was official. The day had been a deep dark one. An innocent telephone conversation to my mother had ruined a

I Told You Not To Climb The Cactus

promising start. Someone needs to invent the small portable phone I can carry about in my pocket, I thought despondently.

Wendy Hamilton

Kids Clothes.

It is a blessing that children do not stay small forever. Eventually, I was able to work on Friday mornings in the Antiques and Collectables shop next door. Once a year there was an Antiques Show. It was held in the buildings of the local sports stadium. One such weekend, my boss and I worked hard on Friday to set up a booth. The next morning Jill and I waited in anticipation. Suddenly the doors opened and the serious collectors swarmed in, hoping for something unique. By lunchtime, however, the frenzy was calming down as casual buyers replaced the serious ones. A woman radiating French perfume strolled over to our stall.

"Hello, Wendy, how are you?"

"Fine," I smiled, acting as if I knew her.

"How is the show going?"

"Very good," I replied, my mouth on autopilot. My mind, however, was going a million miles an hour.

Who is she? I thought frantically. She knows my name so I must know her. I trawled through my memory. Sadly,

I Told You Not To Climb The Cactus

the only thing I dredged up were question marks. I can't admit that I have no idea who she is, I thought anxiously, as I watched the mystery woman finger an expensive figurine. I'll fake it, I thought, hoping that time might shed light on her identity.

"Lladro, do beautiful work," she said putting the figurine down.

"They certainly do," my mouth agreed.

She examined a Spode platter while I continued my internal monologue.

It seems so dishonoring not to know her, I thought. After all, who wants to be forgotten. Besides, it might wreck a sale if I blurt out "who the heck are you?"

We chatted as we drifted around the booth. I noted from the corner of my eye that Jill had just sold the art-deco tea trolley. She chattered as the customer paid and took the large cheque as if it were a detail that almost escaped her attention. Later, away from the public eye, we would exult over it. That sale alone made the weekend worthwhile.

My mystery woman put the platter back on an English-sideboard and turned her attention to the embroidered doilies.

"I remember your girls in the garden wearing those lovely pinafores, they looked so nice."

The fog in my mind lifted. This lady was one of the many pedestrians I chatted to over my front fence.

"That goes back a few years, Doreen," I said. "Marie and Hannah are in their twenties now. Funny you should mention those old pinafores, I saw one of them on an unknown child the other day. The navy-blue corduroy has turned pale blue. They must be about fifteen years old now. I think most of the home-schooling families around here have received them as hand-me-downs at some time or other," I laughed.

"The embroidery was so nice," my friend commented as she picked up an embroidered doily.

I smiled. I knew those pinafores had survived this long because of my handwork and that made me feel good. Unlike the corduroy fabric, the rich hues of French knots and bullion roses remained bright.

My friend bought a doily and drifted out. Her scent lingered for a few minutes. Her words, however, remained much longer. They were still with me at the end of the day. How well I remembered those pinafores and the guilt that inspired them.

"Our girls look revolting," I said to Ian one afternoon many years ago. "Their hair is straggly and half the time they have sticky faces and hands."

"God looks on the heart," quoted Ian breezily. He was not squeamish about grubby looking kids.

"Yes, but man looks on the outward appearance," I said, quoting the first part of the Bible verse.

That was the problem in a nutshell. I could not see the ethereal hearts of my children through the wall of visual unattractiveness.

"I feel guilty," I admitted to my husband when the girls were well out of earshot.

"Why?"

"You know that old saying a face only a mother could love?"

"Of course."

"Well, sometimes I look at our messy kids and don't feel love. In fact (if I'm going to be really honest) sometimes I feel like I loathe them."

"You don't really," said Ian comfortingly.

I Told You Not To Climb The Cactus

"I suppose so," I sighed unconvinced. I turned the phrase man looks on the outward appearance over in my mind. I thought of my husband's reaction to my confession. If man looks on the outward appearance, how much more do women; and in particular, this woman.

"I think I need to do something about this," I said firmly.

"Good for you," encouraged Ian. "Do I have time to mow the lawn before dinner?"

"Yes," I replied walking into the bathroom. "Come in here girls," I called down the hallway.

Their small bare feet made a thundering sound as they ran across the wooden floor.

I rinsed out a flannel and started scrubbing Marie's face vigorously.

"You're hurting," she squealed trying to twist away.

"Hold still," I admonished, lightening up a little with the wash-cloth. "Now hold out your hands."

She held them out obediently.

"I don't know how you kids get so sticky and dirty," I grumbled, cleaning between her fingers. I gave one last wipe and let her go. I turned my attention to Hannah and started on her face. As if she was allergic to cleanliness, Hannah sent up a wail.

"Stop it Hannah and Marie, don't run off, I'm not finished with you yet," I halted my daughter as she moved towards the door. I rubbed the last speck of grime from Hannah's fingers and let her go. "Stand over there in the light where I can see you easily," I instructed, pushing them towards the brightest corner of the room. They shuffled over unenthusiastically.

"Hmmm, I eyed the hair critically, even clean and combed it looked messy

Wendy Hamilton

"Long hair for children is out," I decided. I rummaged in the bathroom cabinet and pulled out a pair of scissors. Marie's overgrown fringe came down to her nose. Snip, snip went the scissors and a fine set of eyes popped out. Snip, snip and the straggles fell to the floor in golden heaps. Then it was Hannah's turn. When I was finished, the small bobbed heads looked charming with their simple hairstyles.

I turned my attention to my children's clothes. Why did they always look bad, regardless of how much effort I put into making them tidy? Cartoon characters plastered over the girl's chests did not improve the look. Graphic tee-shirts are out, I decided firmly. Belly buttons exposed by slipping skirts looked even worse. I pulled the skirts up, aware that it was a futile action; five minutes on the trampoline and the waistband would be around their hips again. I focused on the problem.

"Hmmmmm?" Light-bulb! Kids have no waists. A skirt on the little girl is like a tire on a greasy telephone pole; there is nothing to hold it up. I remembered the clothes I wore as a child. Little tartan skirts always hung from a cotton bodice and were covered by a blouse and a sweater.

"You can go now girls," I said releasing them. Already they looked heaps better despite their messy clothes. My revulsion had dropped dramatically.

"Ian, where did you put all the old class photos?" I yelled out the window.

He looked up from cleaning the lawnmower. "They're in the hall cupboard in a wooden bread box."

I scooted down the hall, whisked the cupboard door open, and lifted out the box and carried it to the kitchen table.

"Here we go," I said aloud to the empty room as I found several 1960s class photos. I studied them closely. All the

I Told You Not To Climb The Cactus

girls looked tidy because not one skirt relied on the vain hope of an elastic waistband.

The next day, armed with my new knowledge and a bolt of fabric, I set about designing winter pinafores.

A gathered skirt attached to a front and back bib will do the trick, I thought. If I make the shoulders and waist adjustable, that will allow for growth. I cut out six of everything and zoomed them up on my sewing machine. When they were finished, I added the embroidery to the bibs purely for the pleasure of doing it. With a blouse underneath and room to grow up and out, my girls wore those pinafores for many years. I even prolonged their life by adding a deep frill around the bottom when the skirts finally got too short. Summer was solved with simple cotton dresses.

My labor was well rewarded. Many women like Doreen lent over my fence and said, "your girls look so nice."

It may be shallow, but I found coping with small children much easier when they looked clean and cute. It was pleasant to feel in one area at least, I was a conquering success.

Until the boys were potty trained, that is. I never solved the problem of low-riding shorts. Somehow, partially buttoned overalls hanging off one shoulder seemed so much worse.

Wendy Hamilton

Waifs and Strays.

My back ached as I tucked the blanket around the sheets. I finished making the bed and straightened up. A woman was standing across the bed from me. We stared at each other silently. She was thirty-two, thin and pale. Her eyes were red-rimmed and she oozed exhaustion. My heart went out to her and I wanted to add her to the long list of waifs and strays that came to my door for solace.

I had a knack for attracting people with problems. I found them in supermarkets, the doctor's waiting room or at church. Street pedestrians who took an interest in my garden, often over time and bit by bit; passed under the rose-covered arch, down the path, onto the veranda, and into the front entrance. From there it was straight through to tea in the kitchen.

Then there was the elderly lady who lived next door. She tried hard to emulate the stray tabby cat who just shifted in without an invitation and took over.

"Pearl is the worst," I complained to Ian. "I feel sorry for

I Told You Not To Climb The Cactus

her. It must be hard being ninety and lonely. But I'm getting really sick of her, she comes so often and stays so long."

"Couldn't you visit her and then you can leave when you want?" suggested Ian.

"I do but she still keeps coming here. The worst of it is she tells me the same old stories over and over. She had a troubled marriage and she can't let it go."

"She won't be able to get up our steps much longer," comforted Ian. She is getting shaky on her legs.

"That's true. She really needs to go into a home. I worry about her."

"Hasn't she got a son?"

"Yes, and he visits every so often."

"Perhaps she could go and live with him."

"No way, she is adamant she is not leaving her house."

My husband was right about Pearl's legs. The day came when she could no longer visit. Unfortunately, it did not stop her from getting on the phone every day.

"Wendy do you think you could be a dear and come and hang out my washing. I've washed a couple of blankets and they are too heavy for me to hang out alone."

I did not mind whipping over the fence to hang out the blankets but I resented the extra hour of Pearl telling me,

"and she said and then I said and he took off and I was left…"

I would listen with half an ear waiting for a break in the monologue to getaway. All the while, horrible noises were escalating in my house over the fence. Only screaming and loud bawling released me.

When Pearl's seventy-year-old son Wicks, bought the adjoining house in front of her, I naively thought my troubles were over.

Wendy Hamilton

Water play

I Told You Not To Climb The Cactus

"It never occurred to me that the monologue of and-she-said and-I said, would expand, now that Wicks is next-door," I said bitterly to Ian. "In addition to all the normal gossip, I get, -and-THAT- WOMAN- said…"

"Who is the woman?" asked Ian mystified.

"That Woman is Betty, Wicks' wife. Pearl is extremely jealous of her. It's a strange sort of marriage, sometimes she is there but mostly she lives in her own house."

"How do you know that?"

I knew because I had met her. She often caught me in the garden and lent over the fence for a natter.

"That mother-in-law of mine she is a right cow, you wouldn't believe what she said…wouldn't you think she could…"

Betty was every bit as bitter and long-winded as Pearl. I stood with the trowel in my hand, a plastic smile plastered across my face. I did not want to hear, but I was too much of a coward to say so. At least Betty did not try to come into my house. Her husband, however, had inherited his mother's straying tendencies. He was at the front door again.

"Just thought you might like a box of fruit I got from the supermarket." He grinned toothlessly at me. Under his shock of white wooly hair and large nose, three day's growth bristled from his face. He wore a dirty checked shirt tucked into saggy trousers tied up with twine.

"That is kind of you," I lied. We both knew it wasn't kind, it was manipulative. Not a single peach was edible. All the reasonable ones were diligently removed by Wicks first. I wanted to shove the whole rotten lot back at the cunning old man and shout,

"I don't want your horrible presents and I don't want you in my house." But of course, I did not. I had been

Wendy Hamilton

well schooled from infancy that, Jesus first, others second, yourself last spells J.O.Y. I had heard it over and over, along with you might be the only Bible your neighbor ever reads.

Well, being a Bible to Wicks was not having a cleansing effect on him. Neither were the excessive visitors putting J.O.Y. into my life.

My location added to the problem. Everyone passed my door weekly for something or other in their ordinary line of business. One did not need to go out of their way to drop in. It was my hometown and I knew a lot of people.

The doorbell was ringing again. I opened it reluctantly.

"Hello, Karren." A young woman with too much time on her hands stood in front of me.

"Hello, Wendy, I'm bored and I had nothing to do so I thought I would come and see you," she said brightly.

I ground my teeth inwardly. I was not bored and had too much to do. I should have fixed her problem by handing her a paintbrush and an overall and given her a job.

"Hello, Karren, nice to see you." (More lies.) Come in and have a cup of tea. I acted as if stopping to talk was what I most wanted to do.

She stayed all morning and we talked about nothing of importance. By the time she left, I felt so depleted I had no energy for painting the veranda.

Things were spiraling out of control and my little children were getting the dregs of my attention. Marie was exceptionally perceptive. The day I saw her try to protect me from yet another visitor, was the day I decided things had to change. They all had to go. Pearl and Wicks, the pedestrians, the I-am-bored brigade, and the I-have-a-problem crowd. The only two that could stay were the tabby cat and the distressed woman looking at me from across the bed. She

I Told You Not To Climb The Cactus

was the only troubled woman I should keep. I knew exactly how she felt and what she needed. Moreover, there was no one in the world other than me who could help her. The idea took urgent hold. I would make room for her in my life from now on. I smiled at her and the woman in the mirror smiled back at me.

Wendy Hamilton

The Transformation.

I am told you can turn coal into diamonds if you apply enough pressure. Cowardice can be turned into bravery by the same principle.

"It's easy deciding to cut visitors down. Doing it is quite another matter," I wailed to Ian.

"You will have to say, I'm sorry but I can't talk when the phone rings or visitors call," said Ian sensibly. It was good advice, but I was too much of a coward to actually say it.

"I'll pray about it," I answered evasively. In my heart, I knew it was a cop-out; prayer is a powerful tool provided it is not used to avoid necessary confrontation. I started by laying yellow hands on the telephone.

"Please, Lord don't let anyone call me except my mother and husband. And Lord, no visitors this week, please. Amen."

Simultaneously, the telephone and the doorbell rang.

I Told You Not To Climb The Cactus

So much for that! I welcomed my visitor with the phone tucked between my shoulder and cheek. Inwardly I was disappointed with God.

"Come in, come in, I won't be long, take a seat I'll put the kettle on."

I smiled falsely at my guest as I ushered her into the kitchen.

"Oh, is that right," (into the phone.) "Uh huh…….. mmmmmm…….really……no…….um….. Could I call you back I've got someone here? ……..Thanks, I'll give you a call later, bye-bye."

I made the tea to the background tune of, "and he said ………. and then I said…….. And then you will never guess what she did!……. Wouldn't you think she could have……"

A loud rapping on the front door interrupted the gossip session. "Excuse me," (to my visitor). I could see the shadow of two figures through the frosted glass of the front door. I cracked it open nervously and peered around the edge like an old lady expecting thugs. Despite the two women being strangers, I knew who they were.

"Hello, we are from the Religious Tract Society and we are in your area this morning. The world is getting more dangerous and evil every day ………." The speaker dug in her bag for a magazine.

I knew where this was going and I wanted to say "I'm not interested and I don't want a magazine." But instead, I stood glued to the doorstep, listened to the whole patter and accepted a magazine.

In the fullness of time they left. I shut the door behind them and headed back down the hallway to my visitor seated at the kitchen table. Halfway down I was waylaid by the shrill sound of the phone. I picked it up.

Wendy Hamilton

"Hello…………yes."

Knock, knock, knock.

"Could you hang on a minute someone is knocking at the door?"

I opened the door once again and waved another woman down to the kitchen.

"Um…..I've got a couple of people here could I call you back?" I said into the phone.

It was late afternoon before I got the women out of my house and dealt with all the back calls. It had been an abnormally crazy day. The visitors had poured in and the phone had jangled with the frequency of a chiming clock. I shut the front door and slid down the frosted glass panels into a heap on the floor. The entranceway was littered with toys and the kids were running amuck in the adjacent front room. I wondered wearily what else had deteriorated while I was preoccupied with Mrs. Time-Waster and her cronies. I felt angry with God.

"You know I'm neglecting my kids because of all these uninvited visitors and callers. Why don't you answer my prayers? Why have you let this be the worst day of all? You know I am at breaking point," I cried out to Him in anguish. "Why are you letting me go through all this?"

"So, you will get desperate enough to change." The quiet words dropped into my mind and seeped into my heart with the conviction of truth.

I looked at my wrecked house. I looked at my naughty girls jumping on the beds. Ian was due home. The dinner should have been on, the washing taken in, and the kids bathed.

How had my life got so out of control?

I knew the answer. I was afraid to say no. I was a people

I Told You Not To Climb The Cactus

pleaser and I did not want to disappoint anyone.

I thought of an early afternoon caller. She was angry with God because her life was not going the way she wanted it to. I thought about my own anger and disappointment over God's refusal to silence my phone and stop the visitors. God, Himself was not above disappointing people; often he said no. I was attempting to be bigger than God. And in trying to be everything to everyone who asked something of me, I was failing in my primary responsibilities.

"There is not enough of me to go around. Somebody has to be disappointed," I said to a spider on the wall, "the big question is, who?"

I dug around and found a thimbleful of courage. I pulled it up from the pit of my stomach and felt strength rise through the core of my inner being. When it reached my shoulders, I threw them back and marched out to the garage. In the firewood pile, I found a short board. It would do the job. I grabbed a hammer and a pot of black paint.

"Now where did I put my sable paintbrushes?"

When Ian arrived home, something was new. Nailed to the gate under the rose-covered arch, was a sign, It said *Visitors by Appointment Only*.

The sign on the gate was small. The change in my heart was big.

It is not easy for a coward to become brave, the God who created diamonds, however, knows just how much pressure to apply.

Wendy Hamilton

A Good Deal.

"You're the woman who lives in the house with the sign on the gate!" said the checkout girl. She stared at me curiously, glad to get a close look at such an oddity.

I cringed. Nobody knew me anymore as the lady who made amazing quilts. Or even as the mother of the two little girls who lived in the cute cottage covered with wisteria. I had a new identity. I was 'The Strange Woman who had the sign on her gate'. How ironic that my fear when I first nailed it in place, was that no one would take any notice of it. It was certainly working. My visitors had dropped significantly. Moreover, I had stopped answering the phone. I still felt tired but at last, I had time to oversee my home properly.

I put my groceries away, still wondering how the checkout girl knew about me. I opened the fridge and realized it needed a good clean. How wonderful to have some energy to deal with it. I took everything out, rinsed the veggie bin and wiped the racks. It was nice to have time to catch up on some of the jobs that had slipped behind.

I Told You Not To Climb The Cactus

"You should have been thrown out long ago," I said to the end of a brown cabbage and six dishes of leftovers.

"Mummy there is a lady outside who wants you," Marie's voice interrupted my contemplation of the tomato sauce bottle.

"Why does nobody ever put the top back on? It makes such a mess when it falls over," I muttered in a preoccupied voice. "What did you say, Marie?" I asked surfacing.

"There is a lady outside who wants you."

I dried my hands on my apron as I walked down the hallway. The front door was open but there was nobody there.

"She's by the gate," said Marie pointing under the archway. Sure enough, there was Mary Jane leaning over the picket gate. Her stomach and the words Visitors-By-Appointment-Only kissed each other. In spite of their close lingering embrace, she and the sign had obviously had a big battle. While the sign manfully stalled progress (to the point the latch had not yet been lifted) it was only a matter of minutes before the gate gave way if it did not receive backup.

"Hi Wendy, I was passing and had nothing to do so I thought I would drop in and see you," called Mary Jane over the short expanse of lawn between the gate and the front veranda. I gulped but stood firm.

"Sorry Mary Jane, I am not having visitors today."

I watched her face fall and felt pangs of guilt and remorse. She was visibly disappointed. The old patterns reasserted themselves and the words 'don't worry about it, come on in,' arose in my mind and hovered on the threshold of my lips.

"I won't be long." She looked at me expectantly.

Suddenly the wind stopped.

Wendy Hamilton

The pedestrians on the street froze.

The noise of the rushing cars muted.

The trees and the gate leaned towards me, listening.

The world and all heaven held their breath awaiting my answer.

In the suspended silence I thought about boundaries. On the sign Mary Jane's stomach obliterated, I had set a very clear boundary. If Mary Jane received hurt and disappointment by violating it, she had bought the unpleasantness upon herself.

"Not today Mary Jane," I said firmly.

The wind, trees, and pedestrians relaxed. Everything resumed their activity as Mary Jane's stomach and the gate parted company and she moved away.

It was embarrassing to be known around town as 'The-Strange-Woman-with-the-sign-on-her-gate,' but right now because of that, I could go back to cleaning the fridge instead of putting on the kettle. Scrubbing congealed sauce off the bottom shelf seemed delightful compared to a long session of, "and-he-said-and-then-she-said!"

Exchanging pride for freedom is not a bad deal!

I Told You Not To Climb The Cactus

The Sign Again.

It was the day of my sister-in-law Elizabeth's wedding. The ride to the church had turned ugly and the focus was on me. I cowered in the back seat trapped behind my mother-in-law and looked at her hat. It was an impressive creation and certainly marked her out as the mother of the bride. Under different circumstances, I would have enjoyed it exceedingly. It wasn't the color that bothered me, it was the feathers. Until that moment, I had no idea feathers could express deep disapproval.

If only I had sat behind the driver. It would not have stopped the lecture but I could have avoided the feathers. Every indignant jerk of Joan's neck was magnified by the fluffy millinery above me.

The trouble was all to do with the sign on my gate. How the heck did she get to know about it? For crying out loud we live six hours away!

"And *what* about *Auntie Diane*?" continued my mother-in-law in full flight. "*What* if *she* passes through Whangarei and sees the sign?"

I did not know who Auntie Diane was, or why it would be so terrible if she did not call in. As neither of Ian's parents had a sister called Diane, she certainly was not related. But as the feathers were nodding in such a scandalized way, I said nothing. I merely slunk lower in my seat.

The distance to the church was short, but not short enough by far. I leaned against my husband for comfort and wished we had hired a car for the weekend. Miss. Two-Year-Old sat on his knee and Miss. Four-Year-Old-Mouth sat on the other side talking to her Poppa. For once in my life, I wished she might talk louder.

Ecclesiastes states, *there is a time for everything*. Now was the time for a rip-roaring screaming tantrum, and seeing as I couldn't throw it, Marie could do me a favor and really let go. She could have one of those horrible scenes that she so liberally unleashed on me. I looked at her hopefully, but the little spoilsport just sat there angelically. Even Ian who was talking to his father was unaware of my isolated state.

By the time we entered the church, I was not only 'The-strange-woman-with-the-sign-on-her-gate,' I was 'The-inhospitable-daughter-in-law-who-lived-in-the-North.'

"What is it about that little sign, that is getting me into so much trouble?" I asked Ian in the privacy of our room after the wedding. "What is so bad about requesting people to call before dropping in?"

"It's unusual in our culture," said Ian. "People always react to the unusual."

"True," I agreed lethargically. "But seriously, six-hundred miles? That is a long way for its reputation to spread!"

I Told You Not To Climb The Cactus

"And what about Aunty Diane?"

Wendy Hamilton

"Don't look at me," said my husband shrugging his shoulders, "I didn't tell anyone about it."

"I could have done without this battle," I said in a wobbly voice. "Just getting here has taken all my strength. If I had put the sign up a year ago, maybe I would have had the energy to actually enjoy Elizabeth's wedding. I couldn't have made it here without you," I said leaning against him.

Mind-numbing exhaustion was really setting in. I could feel my energy scraping across the gravelly floor of rock-bottom. There is an awful line in exhaustion where you stand on the edge of sanity and know it would not take much to fall into the abyss of madness below. I had frittered my emotional reserves away with time-wasters and now I was almost a walking zombie. If anything had gone wrong, I had no coping skills left. While the sign had helped by cutting down casual callers, I was still constantly tired and felt like an elephant was sitting on my chest.

I was burned out.

The wisest thing I ever heard about burnout is, expect it to take as long to get out of as it took to slide into it. I could also add, expect battles when you change course and sail against the current.

"Why can't everyone just accept my *no* like Mary Jane?" I asked Ian after the wedding in the privacy of our room.

"People don't like being told no," said Ian.

"Your dead right about that," I agreed, thinking of all the people I had offended by saying no.

"At least offended people won't want to see you," teased Ian.

"Yeah, they're better than Felicity who just ignored me and came on Friday as usual," I agreed with a weak smile. "But now your mother is having a go at me!" I finished

I Told You Not To Climb The Cactus

feeling sorry for myself.

"try to keep out of her way," said Ian.

It was good advice but not easy to do while we stayed in her house. I am not sure how I ended up alone in the basement with Joan. It was the worst possible place. She was attacking me again and there was no one to rescue me.

Just focus on the peaches and tune her out, I thought desperately. I stared at the rows of beautiful preserves and remembered my husband's stories. Stories of pinching peaches and eating them under the house. But it was no good. They were comforting but not comforting enough. How had I allowed myself to get in this situation under the stairs, alone with no hope of escape?

"And *what* if *Auntie Diane* had been passing through Whangarei and *seen* the sign!"

There it was again. Auntie Diane and the sign!

Suddenly something deep within me rose up. I did not care if Auntie Diane saw the sign. I did not care if I never saw her. In fact, that would be great! I did not care two hairs what Auntie Diane thought about me. And even more importantly, it did not matter if my mother-in-law disapproved of me. There was too much at stake to bow to people pressure. I drew myself up.

"Joan, I don't care if Auntie Diane never calls," I said firmly. "My kids have been getting the dregs through too many visitors. I don't care if I offend Auntie Diane, or you, or the whole world. I will do whatever I need to protect my kids. *I am not taking down that sign!*"

As I started talking, my voice grew louder and stronger and more intense. And as the passion poured out of me a curious thing happened. The room and the bottled peaches and the basement staircase seemed to fade, until there was

Wendy Hamilton

just Joan and me. And as I grew and Joan subsided, her lips turned up and her eyes twinkled. I was not wearing a hat with feathers but we both knew who the victor was.

"Fair enough," she said backing down.

It occurred to me that used sparingly, a bit of Viking blood can bring reassurance to in-laws that you are up to the job of looking after their grandkids. I went back upstairs with new confidence. I had won the battle.

We flew home the next day and the controversial little sign that stirred up so much trouble stayed on the gate. Many months later, however, it disappeared. I never made another one as I did not need it anymore. I suppose some teenage boy stole it and hung it on his bedroom door to annoy his mother. I know from experience it's inflammatory quality would exceed his wildest hopes.

I Told You Not To Climb The Cactus

Wet Weather.

It was unseasonably wet. It had rained solidly for two weeks and the weather forecast darkly hinted at a possible further two weeks of rain. The back lawn had disappeared under water and reeds were sprouting where grass once grew. Even trees have their limits. The big old grapefruit tree had drowned. It stood stiffly like a huge dried arrangement. Unlike the dried roses and lavender that hung from my kitchen mantle, however, it did not beautify the surroundings.

I stared at the dense silver curtain on the other side of the windowpane and my mouth drooped. The garage was already packed with closely strung cords, chocked full of little clothes; they hung like lumpy Tibetan prayer flags that did not bring peace.

I sniffed.

There was an unpleasant odor. It had been growing over the last few days. The week-old sweaters had passed their dry-by-date. Like the half-price-for-a-quick-sale cheese in the supermarket, the mold was setting in. They would all have to be soaked and re-washed. I thought of the growing pile of laundry spilling out of the dirty-washing-basket. If this kept up much longer, the washing machine would be buried under a mountain of grubby clothes. Too bad we did not have the money for a drier.

I sighed. Today had all the signs of a bad day and the kids were not even up yet.

How was I going to occupy them?

The play-dough, coloring in, story tapes, and 'Mother and Father' games had been done to death. The wooden clothes horse draped with blankets, had been a hut in the bedroom longer than I could stand. Wet raincoats and sodden gumboots steamed in the back entrance. The idea of putting the clammy things on and sloshing down to the muddy park again was revolting. (There is a limit of stale bread in any house and only so much duck watching anyone can stomach.)

They could float in the lid of the sandpit, I thought suddenly; the yellow clam-shell had been a huge hit. Emptied of sand, it made a fabulous flat-bottomed boat.

But do I really want to drag that thing around the backyard/pond?

The answer was a resounding NO. They can badger their father for that treat. Besides anything that might increase wet clothes is strictly out!

I considered rolling up the hallway runner and letting them slide up and down the polished wood.

No, that would be better saved for just before bedtime. It would hasten sleepiness; especially if I coupled it with the threat of bed as soon as they stopped running.

My feet plodded about the house looking in cupboards and toy baskets for inspiration.

I Told You Not To Climb The Cactus

I opened my closet, but the only thing that caught my attention was my wedding dress hanging in the furthest part of the recess. My hat and veil sat on the shelf above it.

No, I will *never* let them dress up in my wedding clothes, I vowed, thinking of my mother's lovely dress we three kids ruined. It was not designed to stand up to the rigors of dress-ups.

"Why did we think the heavy satin brocade dress would be suitable attire for Tarzan?" I asked my sister whenever we reminisced.

"I dunno." Antoinette was also perplexed. "Back then it seemed entirely logical that Tarzan should swing across the creek wearing it."

"Come to think of it, why were we playing Tarzan at all?" I asked.

My sister's perplexed expression deepened. "I have no idea….. No wait…" her face lit up with a light bulb shaft of illumination. "Don't you remember the TV program and our rope-swing by the creek?"

"Oh yeah, that explains the Tarzan bit. Why did he need to do it wearing a lace veil?"

"You got me there," said Antoinette, the perplexed look returning.

"It's a crying shame we dragged that elegant train through the creek," I mused, revisiting our childhood actions through the lens of adulthood.

"Don't forget that Rubella got the veil caught in the holly bushes that grew along the bank," Antoinette reminded me.

"I remember now! Those prickly leaves were murder to stand on with bare feet."

"They were even more disastrous to the veil," mumbled Antoinette darkly.

Wendy Hamilton

"What happened to it in the end?"

"Mum threw it and the dress out. They weren't fit for rags by the time we had finished with them."

"Just as well none of us wanted to get married in our mother's wedding dress," I said. "I wonder why our mother let us ruin it?"

"Can't answer that one," said Antoinette. "I'll tell you one thing though, my kids are *never* getting *my* wedding dress!"

"I couldn't agree more."

A shriek rent the air. The ominous sound of escalating noise pulled me back to my quest. Next to the hat sat a large glass jar filled to the brim with buttons. I looked at it speculatively. Suddenly I had an inspiration. After breakfast and the chores, the kids could string button necklaces. I hunted about and found a reel of fishing nylon.

That will work, I thought. I flexed a strand and tested it for rigidity. *Nice;* it was thin enough to poke through the eyeholes, yet stiff enough to do so without a needle. I cut a length from the reel, slipped a button on and tied it firmly to the end. Hopefully, that would keep them occupied for a bit. Meanwhile, the noise from the front bedroom had deteriorated into raucous laughing and yelling. I prepared another string hastily. Unfortunately, I would have to let them get up, six-thirty in the morning and already I had Cabin-fever.

"OK you kids can get out of bed and come and have some breakfast," I yelled down the hallway.

It was not a lovely Hollywood greeting. I did not go in there and tenderly kiss my kids and say, *rise and shine sleepyhead.* Neither did I slide open the curtains with a flourish and say, *"it's another beautiful day,"* because it

I Told You Not To Climb The Cactus

certainly was not.

The girls catapulted out of bed and rushed down the hallway into the kitchen. I could see by their squirrel-like energy, that they had been struck down with a bad case of Cabin-Fever.

Cabin-fever is not listed in medical dictionaries, although it should be. This dreadful affliction is usually triggered by wet weather. Although adults and children easily succumb to the malady, it hits adults harder.

Symptoms in kids include, escalating energy which acts as a stimulus to rambunctious activities, especially if there is more than one child involved. As the disease progresses, one can expect to see a rapid rise in noise, hilarity, silly twaddle and activities injurious to the health of your furniture.

Adults by contrast, suffer a marked decrease in energy accompanied by a deepening awareness of a lack of wellbeing. For adults, there is also an increase in noisiness. But this does not include hilarity or anything remotely related to light-heartedness. If the adult involved happens to be the mother of the affected children, she will also suffer guilt. While this is an ever-present occupational hazard, the levels in her system will steadily increase proportionally to the unraveling of her self-control. Any woman, who claims to still be holding it together after several wet weeks cooped up with small children, has an additional problem. She is a liar.

This is my fourteenth day of rain. I have severe Cabin-fever and my temper can be triggered by a hair.

The button idea works well. I have a ten-minute reprieve, which I spend at the other end of the house as far away from the stringers as I can get. There is a thundering sound as they hurtle down the hallway looking for me.

Wendy Hamilton

My kids are never getting my wedding dress

I Told You Not To Climb The Cactus

What a pity all good things come to an end.

"Look at what we made," they shout.

I tie the lumpy button snakes together at the ends and slip the necklaces over the heads of my feverish children.

"Oh, don't you look lovely," I say mechanically.

They smile and preen themselves in the mirror which gives me an idea.

"Why don't you get the dress-up-bag and play dress ups?"

They are excited, but only if I add something new to the well-used assortment.

"Can we play with your wedding dress?"

I remember the murder of my mother's special dress.

I think of my vow.

I look at the eager faces and speculate on how many hours reprieve it could buy.

I have a flash of insight and I know for sure how my sisters and I got possession of our mother's wedding dress. And that I also will not leave a legacy for brides to hand down the generations. That sort of sentimentality is reserved exclusively for women who live in a dry climate.

"You can play with the hat and shoes today," I say with resignation.

"Next week if it is still raining, you can have the dress."

Wendy Hamilton

The Tyrant and the Slaves.

I gave one last wipe to the sink bench and looked around the kitchen in satisfaction. The house felt clean and orderly, time to relax with a cup of tea and enjoy the fruit of my labor.

I wonder what the kids have been doing in my absence, come to think of it, they have been very quiet, just a few thumps and bangs. The more I thought about it, the more the continuing silence seemed ominous, time to investigate.

I strode purposefully down the hallway. The front bedroom door was closed (another red flag) as was the subdued giggling. I pushed open the door. What I should have seen, was two neatly made beds in a tidy room; that was the way I had left it two hours ago. What I saw instead, was toys and sheets scattered all over the room and an empty space where the second bed should have been.

"What is going on?" I thundered.

I Told You Not To Climb The Cactus

"We're making bunks," a cheeky little voice piped up. The four-year-old looked at me perkily while her two-year-old accomplice peeked out from behind her unquenchable sibling. I looked at the size of the two single beds stacked messily on top of each other. I looked at the size of the laborers. The contradiction of small size and great strength did the logical side of my brain in. It just did not compute. But then many people had expressed the same surprise about me.

It must be the ancestry of those tough little Shetlanders surfacing, I thought. I felt a rush of that Viking heritage inject venom into my own bloodstream.

"You put back those beds this instant and straighten up this room." I commanded. "I want to see all the toys back in the toy-box. You have twenty minutes. I want it done before the buzzer rings," I finished as I wound up a kitchen timer. I stomped back down the hallway and retrieved my now tepid cup of tea.

In the lounge, I slumped into my favorite armchair. I did not relax, however, neither did I enjoy the pleasant room. At Yummo Pies (where we sometimes went for a treat) there was a slide that catapulted kids into a pit of multi-colored plastic balls. As I sat there, I visualized those balls all caught up in a net.

"One slash with a knife an all those balls fall instantly to the floor," I said aloud to the empty room. "It would take a lot more effort to pick them all up again," I continued morosely. "I bet Murphy had some sort of law concerning this phenomenon."

The same one-way system was in progress down the hallway. I knew when the buzzer rang, that tidy order would *not* greet me when I investigated. The twenty minutes was for me to calm down and think. I thought for ten minutes without getting past the stuck record of, "raising kids is the pits, raising kids is the pits!"

Suddenly I had a better thought. I need to pray.

"Lord, please help, I am about to blow my stack, I feel so angry."

The twenty minutes were nearly up before I had a shaft of heavenly insight.

You can't afford the luxury of doing everything yourself. The thought dropped into my mind and I knew it was not my own wisdom.

"But it will take so much longer," I argued.

A child engaged in cleaning up a house will not have the time to tear it down.

I thought of the shenanigans escalating in the front room and knew the words were true. I straightened my shoulders, launched purposely out of the chair, and strode through to the bedroom. As I expected, nothing had improved.

"I think it is high time you girls learned to make your beds," I said.

"Take the other end of the bed," I commanded, pointing to the top 'bunk.'

Marie shuffled over while Hannah pretended not to hear me.

"You too Hannah, you were part of this," I said poking her towards the bed. "That's right, take one leg each."

"It's heavy," wailed Marie.

"Don't try that on me," I said ignoring the wail. "You managed to get this bed up here by yourself so you can certainly get it down with the help of your sister," I said snappily. "Lift it down on the count of three. One, two, three."

I Told You Not To Climb The Cactus

There was a thump as four wooden legs hit the floor. I pushed the bed back into place against the wall. "OK kids, I want each of you to pick up a sheet and put it on your bed."

The girls looked at me as if I was speaking Swahili.

"Hurry up, stop twirling around Marie. And Hannah, put the cat down."

"Where is the sheet?" asked Marie stalling.

"You're standing on it," I said irritated.

She bent down and picked up an end.

"You too Hannah. Now spread it evenly over the mattress."

Marie started to half-heartedly pull the sheet onto her bed with one hand.

"Put Fiona down. You can't work while you hold a doll in your hand."

"I need to go to the potty," said Hannah.

"You can't possibly, you went not long ago. Hurry up and put the sheet on your bed."

Hannah meandered over to her bed trailing a sheet behind her.

"Quickly, we don't have all day." I helped my children straighten and tuck in the bottom sheets.

"Now we are going to put the top sheet on."

Marie stared out the window disinterestedly while Hannah picked up a Teddy Bear.

"Look at me Marie. I want you to pay attention when I am talking and Hannah, put that Teddy bear down."

They obeyed slowly.

"I said the sheet Marie, not the floor rug. Get it off your bed........."

It was one o'clock in the afternoon and the house was almost tidy. It had been two weeks since the 'bunks' fiasco and we were still getting used to the new routine. I gave the shoddily cleaned bench a decent wipe and scooped up the crusts Marie had missed with the broom. The girls watched me anxiously.

"All right, that will do," I said releasing them. "You can play quietly in your room. But remember, any mess you make, *you* will be cleaning up. I'll make lunch in a minute."

They raced off before I could change my mind.

I made a cup of tea and staggered into my almost clean lounge for a well-earned break.

As I sipped tea, I thought of my childhood and remembered all the times I accused my mother of only having kids so she could have unpaid maids. An old memory surfaced. I remember slipping past her swinging a feather duster.

"I have finished dusting the house," I said confidently.

"I could not have dusted that fast!" she replied unimpressed by my efficiency.

It has taken me all these years to realize she was not excessively slow, and why that was not a compliment.

I thought of the sacrifice that house-proud woman made by insisting I do the dishes and clean my room. On impulse I picked up the phone.

"Hello," my mother answered.

"Hello, Mum, remember all those times we were at loggerheads and I called you a slave-driving tyrant?" I asked.

"Vaguely," she replied. (Time has a way of softening memories.)

"I just want you to know I now think the real villain was your three-foot opponent. Thank you, Mum, for teaching me and resisting the secret temptation to send me to an orphanage!"

I Told You Not To Climb The Cactus

Prams, Strollers and Pushchairs.

The nicest mode of transport is a pram; not even a train is as good. When I was small, my grandmother used to load my sister and me into a huge cane pram and push us to the park. The fact I remember it suggests that I was rather old to still be enjoying this luxurious pleasure. I was, however considerably younger than ten, which is the age I finally stopped playing with it. My cousin Paul was the most adventuresome. While the rest of us squeezed into its cavernous depths and pretended to be big babies, Cousin-Paul's greatest fun was to torment his younger sister. He roared her around the streets in it like a go-cart on steroids; bouncing down culverts and zooming along gutters.

"The best time was when he ran off leaving Lynette stranded in the middle of the busy main road," said my sister when we were reminiscing one day.

"Yeah," I agreed callously. "I still remember Lynette

sitting in the pram on the centerline, bleating, *Paul, Paul, don't leave me in the middle of the road!"*

"Why didn't she just get out and push it to the other side?" asked Antoinette.

"Beats me," I said. "My memory is getting a bit fuzzy. Perhaps he had tied her in."

"Yes, that would be possible," she agreed, thinking of the small rings at the side of the pram and Cousin-Paul's mischievousness.

"It's a wonder those wheels never popped off, he was so rough with them," I mused.

"We were all rough with them," corrected my sister.

She was right. My first stroller would not have coped with the punishment we meted out to the old cane pram. Stroller-number-one was lightweight and folded down into little more than an umbrella. It rolled smoothly on whirly wheels the size of jumbo-cookies. Moreover, they swiveled in all directions; the way a horse's eyeballs do when he sees something really scary (like a plastic bag.) The stroller was ideal because the seat could be flattened for a newborn or tilted upright for a nosey toddler.

"Let's try it out," said Ian excited by our new acquisition.

"How are we going to do that?" I asked reasonably. "The baby is still a bump and you and I are too big to sit in it."

Ian looked around the room for a substitute infant. His eye fell upon the slumbering cat.

"Perfect," he crowed, scooping up the big stripy tabby. Nearby sat a fully equipped baby-bag and the pile of tiny clothes I had gathered in preparation for our firstborn. He swooped down on them and whisked a stretch-n-grow off the top.

I would like to pretend that I was too mature to indulge

I Told You Not To Climb The Cactus

in what happened next. The truth is, however, that childhood patterns asserted themselves and I put up little resistance.

"Hold him down Wend," said Ian working briskly. He thrust the placid cat's legs into the four corresponding apertures in the toweling suit. The tail, however, was problematical.

"Stick it through a hind leg hole," I advised. I had more experience in dressing cats than Ian. Oliver growled slightly but did not strike out as most cats would have. He did not fuss when Ian dumped him into the seat of the stroller either. And merely glowered as I pushed him around the house. Things deteriorated when it was Ian's turn to drive. Those swiveling wheels could do three-sixties and wheelies like you couldn't believe. The cat was not impressed and abandoned ship in the middle of a spin. Ian lunged after him as he leaped and the chair cannoned backward onto the ground. The front wheels of the stroller pointed skyward like a dead cow's legs. Through the cat, we had discovered its weak point.

"We'll have to watch out for that," I said, picking my baby-bag, wet-wipes, and six diapers off the floor. "Obviously this is not designed to carry anything other than a baby."

"It needs some sort of counterbalance," said Ian letting the cat go. Oliver sunk his belly low to the floor and crawled awkwardly under the couch.

"I don't see how you could put a counterbalance on it," I objected. "There's not much to it."

"True," agreed Ian picking it up with one hand easily. He peered at it speculatively. "There is not even any way we could put a tray underneath."

"I suppose it doesn't really matter," I said. "It won't tip over when the baby is in it, which is the main thing. I'll just have to remember to take the baby-bag off the handles before I take the baby out."

And at first that was exactly right, it really did not matter. When Marie arrived, we did not need a tray underneath because we took the car to the supermarket and around town. It was when we brought our first house and the car died the problems started.

"We are not going to be able to afford another car if we want to fix up the house," said Ian staring at a spreadsheet of numbers.

"I'd rather fix up the house than have a car if I have to choose," I said firmly. "Now we live so close to town it is quite feasible to live without a car. We can walk almost everywhere and the supermarket is close."

"I'm glad you feel like that Wend, because so do I," agreed Ian relieved. "We don't both need to go grocery shopping; one of us can stay with Marie and we can use her stroller to carry stuff home."

I eyed the light little stroller critically. In its new status as the family vehicle, it looked fragile.

"Do you think it will be up to it?" I asked doubtfully.

"Let's try it," suggested Ian eagerly. He wrenched open the cupboard door and dragged out a bag of potatoes which he dumped in the seat. "This will be a good test," he added, plopping a large orange pumpkin on top.

"We'd better make it a really good trial," I said as I loaded cans of food into supermarket bags and hung them off the umbrella-hook handles. "If it is going to collapse, I would rather it broke here than in the middle of the road."

"Don't forget the toilet paper," said Ian rushing off. He came back with a twelve pack. "I think they will squeeze in here," he said optimistically. He jammed them between the

I Told You Not To Climb The Cactus

bottom of the seat and the crossover rails that held the four wheels at opposing corners. The vegetables in the seat kept everything upright but the stitched seams were strained by the weight. They bared little thread teeth in smiles that were not happy.

"I don't like the way that the wheels have splayed out," I said nervously.

"The handles don't look too good either," admitted Ian reluctantly, as he tried in vain to straighten the bow out of them.

I chewed my lip in concern. "We will get away with it for a few weeks, but that's stroller's days are numbered," I said critically.

"Hmmm, you might be right," agreed Ian, "keep an eye out for a stronger one."

I found our second vehicle in the Salvation Army thrift store.

"Good choice, this is much sturdier," said Ian jiggling it. The new model was twice the weight of the first stroller. Unlike the little stroller, this one did not fold up. Moreover, it had a bar-handle and non-swivel wheels the size of saucers. Best of all it had a large plastic tray underneath so I wouldn't have to keep picking toilet rolls off the tarmac every time I crossed the road.

"Now we can both go shopping together again," I said happily.

The arrangement worked well until Hannah was added to the family. As I could not push two strollers by myself, and did not want to be house-bound when Ian was a work, I invested in a good-sized ten-year-old pram.

"It's kind of like a bunk bed with a mezzanine floor," said Ian investigating the detachable carrycot.

Wendy Hamilton

"I suppose you *could* call the little seat that sits on top, a mezzanine floor," I chuckled.

"Here you go Marie," said Ian lifting the toddler onto the seat. "How do you like sitting up here?"

"Tuttle?" piped Marie solemnly.

"Yes, Turtle can have a ride too," I interpreted, handing her the bath toy with a retractable head.

"Bubby too?"

"Yes, Bubby can ride in it when she wakes up," I stalled, not willing to wake a sleeping baby for the sake of trying out a new pram.

"Big wheels," approved Ian gently kicking them. They were the size of bread-and-butter-plates and had rubber tires slicked around their metal rims. The handle was strong and the metal tray beneath was robust. As an added bonus, the steel frame boasted a spring-loaded suspension. It made for very smooth trundling; the girls were cushioned from all bumps until a really good special on watermelons busted it.

"We are going to need something much stronger," said Ian looking at the broken springs thoughtfully, "especially now we are remodeling the kitchen."

"Yes," I agreed. "No bells and whistles, pure strength is what we need."

The last-pram was a huge old 1960s model with the strength of a small tractor. The wheels were the size of dinner plates and the handle as thick as the top rail of a steel farm gate. It had a solid metal tray underneath and a detachable carcass the size of a child's coffin. Theoretically it was collapsible, but not in the quick, slick way my first stroller was.

"Have you got your car nearby," asked the secondhand dealer as I paid for it and a large firewood basket that I also wanted. "I'll get a couple of blokes from out the back to lift them into your car."

"I'll be fine, I said breezily.

"You won't manage to get that pram into the car by yourself Luv," said the man looking concerned. "It weighs a ton."

"Oh, I don't have a car," I answered, "this *is* my car." As I spoke, I lifted Marie off her seat and transferred Hannah from the old pram into the new one. Then I stowed the seat in the metal tray below and popped the firewood basket on the pram where the seat would normally sit. "Here you go Marie," I said lifting her into the basket. She squinted at me through the gaps in the cane like a prisoner peering through prison bars.

"I've never seen anything like that before," said the man, scratching his head in surprise.

"Do you have a dumpster out the back that this could go in?" I asked pointing to my former pram. It listed to one side drunkenly.

"Sure," he agreed, "just leave it there and I will see to it."

I drew many looks and a few chuckles as I pushed my burden through town.

"That will do the job well," said Ian when he got home and saw our new transport. "We can get the lumber for the new pantry now."

"If you look after the kids on Saturday, I could get it," I suggested, leaping at the chance to have a break.

"All right," agreed Ian.

On Saturday morning I strode downtown, pushing the empty pram easily. At the window glaziers, I stopped and purchased a pane of glass for a cracked window. I arrived at the timber yard and picked out six wide planks to line the inside of my new pantry. Like the second-hand dealer, the man in charge of the timber-yard assumed I had a vehicle.

"Bring your vehicle over here," he said looking at a nearby van.

"Oh, that's not mine," I corrected him, "this is mine," I patted the side of the pram.

"You won't get six planks on there," he objected his eyebrows shooting up.

"You would be surprised what I can get home on a pram," I assured him confidently. "Just shove them under the handle." I folded the hood down as I spoke.

"There's not a baby in there, is there?" he asked pulling a face.

"No, nothing like that," I assured him. "Only a pane of window glass."

"Oh wonderful," he said in a tone that suggested quite a different emotion.

I grabbed the end of the first plank as he poked it under the handle and pulled it up over the hood. The two ends overshot the length of the pram by a yard each end. "Keep them to one side so there is room for me to get at the handle," I said as we slid the next one on top.

"You really should have a couple of flags tied on that," quipped the man's coworker. By now a small crowd had gathered around the unusual spectacle.

"I don't need flags," I grinned back. "But I do need to strap these on." I pulled a couple of bungee cords out of the bottom tray and stretched them over my load and onto the metal frame.

Six planks were a lot for a pram to move, but the little trooper did not buckle, bow or collapse.

I Told You Not To Climb The Cactus

"This is my car"

Wendy Hamilton

She did not even skip a beat when I bounced her through deep potholes in the gravel driveway. Once we got to the street things moved a little more smoothly as we slid along the concrete footpath. The culverts were a bit problematical and waiting by the lights for the green-pedestrian-man, took a bit of maneuvering to keep from poking out into the traffic. If a toddler in a firewood basket was an unusual load to move, it was nothing compared to what I was toting now.

"You need to register that as an offensive weapon," yelled a joker out the window of a passing car.

A police car slowed down as it passed and I smiled nervously. It would be embarrassing to get a traffic ticket. He merely waved, however, and carried on. I got the load home with no further incidents; and the pantry when it was finished, was great. While it is not customary to renovate a house with a pram, I can tell you for a fact, that with creative thinking, it *is* possible.

Nowadays my children are long past riding in prams, but like Grandma's cane pram, the tractor-of-a-pram is still going strong. The frame (minus the carrycot) is collapsed at the moment and waits patiently for its next assignment.

"OK, everybody," I say to my husband and four teenage kids as they carry a heavy load around the corner of the house. "Lower the sign onto the pram slowly."

There is a lot of groaning and muttering from my enlisted helpers, which I ignore.

"Hang on, you need to turn it around the other way," I cry, halting the process. "We want all the cars to see the words when we push it down the street, it is good advertising."

"*Dad do we have too?*" the kids appeal to their father. "*This is so embarrassing.*"

"Just do what you're told, there is no point arguing with

I Told You Not To Climb The Cactus

your mother over something like this," says Ian in a resigned tone. When you have been married for over twenty years, you know when to let things go.

There is more grunting and grumbling as the sign revolves a half turn.

"You know, this might be my biggest pram removal ever!" I say, excited by the sheer size and audacity of the move. Like the lumber for the pantry, the sign overhangs the pram/trolley by at least a yard either end. The magnificence which eclipses the pantry, however, comes from its vertical proportions. The red surface is at least as big as a queen-size bed and stands taller than me. To top it off, I have painted huge black words on it. It shouts to the passing cars without an apology, "THE LITTLE CHURCH WITH THE BIG GOD."

It is half a mile to its final destination. We have not quite pushed it out of our gate but already we are turning heads and cars are honking.

"This is so awkward," moan my children. "What if someone we know sees us?"

"Stand up straight," I command my cringing brood. "If you have to do something weird, do it with boldness. The world steps aside for someone who knows where they are going and refuses to be intimidated by what others think."

Wendy Hamilton

Birth Order Pitfalls.

Marie's voice floated up the stairway clearly.

"I was the only one of us kids that had a professional birth."

There was a clamor of hot denials as the other three claimed equally professional births. Upstairs the eavesdropping 'professional birth-giver' silently disagreed. The woman in America who gave birth to twenty kids is a professional. I, who only gave birth to four, am an amateur.

"No, no, I was the only one born in a hospital," continued the smug voice. "All you lot were born in the lounge or the kitchen. When *I* was born, there were doctors and nurses and Mum lay around doing nothing. She was cooking chicken when Hannah was born and baked a banana cake while she was having Joe."

"Hah, hah," sniggered Mark, "Mum didn't cook when I came."

I Told You Not To Climb The Cactus

"No, she didn't," Marie agreed, "she was too busy ordering Dad and the midwife to roll up the floor rug so you wouldn't make a mess on it. That makes me professionally born and all you lot homemade," she finished triumphantly.

Alas it was true, their births deteriorated from Marie (the event of a lifetime) down to Mark (who threatened to leave a stain on my best rug.) Poor Mark, he was also at the bottom of the photograph demise. Every family with multiple children experiences the photograph demise. This is the strange phenomenon where the first child is the subject of a thousand photographs, the second a hundred and the third twenty. Subsequent children can be found at the back of the group in birthday and Christmas photos. I fervently hoped Mark would not be permanently damaged by his mundane birth and lack of photographs. He seemed alright, he was like an Indian-rubber-ball. Somehow, he bounced back up no matter how much his older siblings squashed him.

Down below the silly talk was still in full flight.

Hannah and I had ice cream and fruit salad when Joe was born but you boys missed out, "ha, ha" gloated the thousand-photograph child.

There was a lot more arguing over this inflammatory comment, and snippets of "Mum" and "not fair" floated up. I thought I could hardly be blamed for denying an hour old baby or a nonexistent child ice cream, but I bit back my justification as I did not want to get embroiled in the twaddle going on below.

Marie's mouth was still going but I tuned it out. That mouth had been a thorn in my flesh for many years now. It was a mistake to tell her early that I was expecting Joe. While there was still nothing in my appearance to suggest I was pregnant, six-year-old Marie informed all the supermarket checkout operators, the men in the hardware store, and any pedestrians who passed our gate, "Mum is having a baby!"

It was embarrassing and I felt like a needed to pin a big purple button with the bold yellow words *yes, it is true,* on my chest.

If Marie was professionally born and Hannah and Mark homemade (on account of having turned up in the family home) Joe must, by a similar definition, have been lease-made as he arrived in a rented house. Actually, he was not supposed to have existed for another year but true to his character picked his own time to begin.

"I don't want to shift to Hamilton at all," I told my sister as she helped us pack all our furniture away in the back sunroom. We had been in our own home for four years and the novelty still had not worn off. "I would rather sand and polish the floor."

"It will look gorgeous when it's done," agreed Antoinette. "The wooden floors of these old houses come up beautifully."

"It's only eight months," Ian comforted. "We will be home before you know it."

"I suppose," I admitted. "It is a good thing you can do most of your Master's degree long distance. Eight months is a heap better than three years."

"That's right," said my sister encouragingly. "And you have got great renters."

"That's true," I said. "We couldn't have better ones; especially as it is hard to get short term tenants. Thank goodness, the Grays decided to build a house right now."

I stooped to pick up the end of the heavy rattan couch.

"I'll do that Wend," interposed Antoinette hastily. "You shouldn't be lifting heavy things."

I Told You Not To Climb The Cactus

"I suppose so," I said reluctantly giving way to her. "This is frustrating, getting pregnant right now was not part of the game plan."

"It will turn out alright, you can't always plan these things," puffed Ian as he and my sister carried their burden to the back room. Once there, Ian upended the couch and pushed it hard into the corner.

"Do you want to take this?" asked Antoinette pointing to the beautifully draped bassinet that was so essential for the thousand-photograph baby.

"Nah, we won't have room for it. We are only taking what we can stuff in the van. I'll make do with a bottom drawer or something. The house we are renting is fully furnished." I squished some pink stretch-and-grow suits into a grocery bag and put them in the pile for the van.

"Aren't you expecting to have a boy?" Antoinette asked, shocked by their color.

"It won't matter," I said breezily. "He can wear his sister's hand-me-downs." (What did gender color-coding or a few stains matter to number three.)

Eventually all the furniture was locked away in the backroom and the hired-van was packed.

"Goodbye house," I said sadly as we rolled out the driveway.

"Eight months will pass quickly," said Ian pulling out into a gap in the traffic.

Our new home was a 1950s stucco box opposite a primary school. The house was the property of an old bachelor who lived in the unit behind. Between him and me existed a dispute over the 'fully' part of the definition 'fully furnished.' It was furnished but the lack of fat in the 'fully' part meant I could not spare the traditional bottom

Wendy Hamilton

drawer for a crib. Like Mother Mary, I had nowhere to lay my baby's head when the time drew nigh for Joe to be born.

During one of my regular voyages to the mall, however, I spied a solution. I glided like *'The Endeavor'* in full sail past Baby World and Toys for Tots (who got very hopeful when they saw me) past the ice cream stand (where my kids got hopeful) and round to the back of the Veggie shop. It was the huge mountain of discarded boxes that attracted me.

"Now don't tell the man why I want the box," I hissed at Miss. Thousand-Photograph-Big-Mouth.

I docked close to the most senior worker and leaned on the rowboat of my stroller.

"Do you have an apple box I could have?"

"Have anything you like Luv, take your pick?" the man answered kindly.

There were lots of banana boxes but they were designed with a big hole in the bottom, and the name Banana Baby could stick. Kiwifruit Kid sounded bad too. I spied over in the corner a strong unidentified box just the right shape and depth. Good.

It was a little awkward getting it home on top of the stroller's hood, but well worth it when I surveyed my handiwork a few days later. Draped in blue flannelette with the girl's baby blankets tucked neatly around their old mattress it made a credible bassinet.

Now the only question remaining was, what to do with the girls while I was having the baby?

If we had been back in Whangarei, Mum and Dad would have taken them for a little walk, as they did with Marie when Hannah was born. Home-birth is so non-disruptive. At the critical time, my parents took Marie for ice cream and when they got back, Hannah and I were tidily tucked up in

I Told You Not To Climb The Cactus

bed. Then we all had an afternoon sleep.

Here, however, we knew no one. What were we going to do?

"I don't know why television births are such noisy affairs?" I said to Ian.

"They can hardly have the camera right in the middle of the action," said my husband reasonably. They have to imply birth.

"I suppose that's why there's always a lot of screaming," I agreed, charmed to have a logical explanation for this puzzle. "That will be why her neck is thrown back and the sinews are tight with agony," I mused.

"Why?" asked Ian. (Now he was puzzled)

"It's to imply she's pushing and the baby is being born."

"Oh yeah."

"They always have her in bed. I can't relate to that. I'm more comfy sitting in a chair or moving around."

"I've noticed that," agreed my husband who had observed this phenomenon twice before.

"Why is there much ado about boiling water on television? On screen, it has an anxious medical significance but it was a non-event when our girls were born."

"I think it's because David Copperfield's mother didn't have inside plumbing or electricity," said Ian sensibly. "They probably needed it for baths."

"Or maybe, because Betsey Trotwood was uselessly pacing the floor below instead of rolling up the carpet, the pile of the Persian floor rug needed a good sponging," I said thinking of my own mats. "That would definitely explain the urgency."

While I understand a script writer's temptation to make up a good story, I think the film industry can be held

Wendy Hamilton

responsible for a good deal of the terror young women feel about having their first baby. Unlike Hollywood, I give birth without drama. The thing that shocks my family is cooking not screaming. It is a rare thing for me to bake. The sudden urge to make a banana cake is a sure sign to call the midwife quick. I have heard of other women who clean. You will never see this on TV, however, because a hugely pregnant woman cleaning windows just does not have the same impact. Imagine the difficulty the poor guys making the soundtrack would have. All the violins and kettle drums in the world couldn't make it a nail-biting moment.

Because this birth was not a Hollywood production and the only noise's I make are a few pig grunts at the final crisis, we decided it was feasible to keep the girls at home. When Joe was about to arrive, Ian took them into their bedroom and gave them new coloring books.

"Color Mummy a pretty picture," he said and shut the door.

By the time the girls were ready to show us the fruit of their labor, I was ready to show them the fruit of mine.

Marie had colored her horse pink,

Hannah had colored her bear blue,

And my offering was a mottled red and purple.

After we had admired each of the new creations, we had ice cream and fruit salad to celebrate. The girls remembered quite correctly. Too bad about the floor rug comment when Mark was born, they were not supposed to hear that through the wall and certainly not meant to remember or quote it. It is hard enough being a group-photograph child without being the baby whose mother's first words were, "don't make a mess on my floor!"

I Told You Not To Climb The Cactus

Do Not Climb the Cactus

After the birth of each of our girls, Ian stayed home and looked after me. It was not possible with Joe, however. University life had its pluses and minuses. My husband was home more often but his lectures were inflexible. Ian's parents who lived an hour's drive away came to the rescue.

"Thank you so much for offering to take the girls for two weeks," I gushed with relief when they came over to see the new baby. I handed them each a cup of tea in a jam-jar. "Sorry about the cups," I added pulling a face, "the landlord does not think *fully furnished* runs to cups."

"It doesn't matter," chuckled Wilson.

"Girls get your bags and put them by the car for Nana and Poppa," I said taking a sip of tea. Miss. Big-Mouth was driving me crazy and the sooner she went the sooner I could go back to bed. It seemed to take forever but eventually they were gone.

Wendy Hamilton

"I told you not to climb the cactus"

I Told You Not To Climb The Cactus

"Isn't this nice, you're coming for a little holiday with us," said Nana Joan as the car slid out the driveway.

"Yes," said Marie. "Are we nearly there yet?"

"No poppet, we have a way to go yet," said Nana.

The houses thinned as they left the city boundary?

"Are we there yet?"

"No, honey, we have a long way to go yet. See how many horses you can count."

"There's one," said Poppa Wilson.

"Do you have a cat at your house?" asked Marie disinterestedly.

"No, but we have a dog," answered Poppa.

"Are we there yet?

"Let's play a game called see-who-can-be-the-quietest," said Nana persuasively.

"No, Hannah will win," said Marie looking at her silent sibling.

"Look there is another horse," said Poppa, "it's a spotty one."

"Are we nearly there yet," responded Marie.

"This is going to be a very long trip groaned Nana.

All things come to an end, even an hour-long road trip with a yapping six-year-old.

"Are we nearly there yet?"

"Yes," said Nana with a sigh of relief as Poppa pulled into the bottom of the steep driveway.

The house at the top of the drive was a 1960s weatherboard house that sat high on top of a basement. There was nothing about the house to excite a child. There was something mesmerizing in the garden by the letterbox, however. Marie's attention was so riveted upon the large prickly-pear cactus she went totally silent.

Wendy Hamilton

"Oooo," said Hannah shocked into speech as she stared wide-eyed at the eighth wonder of the world.

Nana's head whipped around and she eyeballed the two small-fry in the back-seat. "Do *not* climb the cactus," she warned in a tone of authority. "*Do you hear me?* Do *not* climb the cactus," she repeated sternly.

Marie, her head twisting further and further around as the car climbed the steep gradient, said nothing. At least she said nothing to her Nana.

"Come on Hannah, Let's go and climb the cactus," she said to her sibling the first chance she had to slip away. Hannah with her thumb in her mouth plodded obediently behind Marie down the driveway.

The cactus at close range was even more impressive. Its big round flaps of flesh looked like large green steps, or so it seemed to Marie. The first step was a perfect height. Marie put her foot on it and started climbing. The cactus bore her weight easily. Hannah at the foot of the cactus watched in silent admiration.

"Look at me, I'm the king of the castle and you're the dirty rascal," sang Marie cheekily.

It was coming down that the problems started. The cactus's sparse long spikes caused no trouble going up. When Marie's legs and bottom brushed against them, they merely yielded. Once she opposed them, however, they reacted more viciously than a wild cat stroked the wrong way.

"Ooooo ow," shrieked Marie sitting on several long spikes as she descended. Hannah sent up a howl of sympathy and the ruckus floated up the driveway.

"Where are the kids?" called Poppa looking up from his paper.

I Told You Not To Climb The Cactus

"I thought they were with you," said Nana coming down the hallway and into the lounge.

"No, I haven't seen or heard them for a while," said Poppa ominously.

"They will be climbing that jolly cactus," exploded Nana, a steely look entering her eye. She bustled down the driveway and stood with her hands on her hips, staring up at Marie. "I *told* you *not* to climb the cactus," she scolded. "Why is it every kid who comes here has to climb the thing?"

"I'm stuck," wailed Marie.

"Hold on, Poppa is bringing the ladder," said Nana. (They had a drill for such an emergency.)

There was a metallic clattering noise as Poppa carried the aluminum ladder down the hill and set it up at the base of the cactus.

"Be careful Wilson, the ground is uneven," said Nana gripping the legs of the ladder as Poppa ascended.

"You're alright," soothed Poppa as he helped Marie off the cactus and onto the ladder. "Hold on tight and follow me down."

Nana was less soothing when she doctored up the damage. "Stop bawling Marie," she commanded as she dug large prickles out of her granddaughter's bottom.

"It hurts," fussed Marie.

Nana, slapping disinfectant on the wounds, had only one thing to say and she said it in a tone tinged with annoyance and frustration.

"*I told you not to climb the cactus,*" she said.

Wendy Hamilton

Little Red Hen's Day of Rest.

Sunday the day of rest. I looked at the kitchen clock in frustration. Eight in the morning; breakfast was over but time was ticking on and I had a lot to do. I could hear the baby crying, as I pulled a clean overall on Joe and brushed his baby curls. The squat toddler sucked his fingers as I hurriedly dressed him. "Go and play with your cars in the lounge," I instructed him, "and don't go outside. Mummy doesn't want you getting all dirty again," I added, straightening his collar. He looked cute as he trundled sturdily out of the room.

I picked up the baby. Fortunately, he was already fed. There was, however, a foul smell radiating from his lower region. I carried the squalling infant over to the changing table and whisked off his dirty diaper. I could see the closed door of the office as I worked. The door was made from solid redwood timber and windowless. Without looking, however, I knew what was on the other side. A quiet, serene

I Told You Not To Climb The Cactus

room and a man sitting undisturbed by domestic trauma. It must be wonderful to be so far removed from motherhood that you could shut yourself away and escape the mammoth task of getting four kids out the door.

I finished changing the baby and buttoned him into a clean stretch-n-grow. Then I pulled a tiny sweatshirt over his head and tied the laces of his booties. At least the youngest two are ready for church, I thought as I lay him on the carpet under a baby-gym. The brightly colored toys dangled above him and he smiled a gummy grin.

"Now where is that baby bag?"

Not where it should be.

"Have you kids been playing with my bag again?" I hollered down the hallway.

"Noooo."

Of course not, I thought sarcastically. Think Wendy think, where could it be? Perhaps Ian tidied it away into the closet? I scooted into the girl's room and opened the wardrobe door. A great avalanche of toys and junk cannoned out all over the floor.

"Marie and Hannah come here," I called. There was no answer. Their Mum's-in-a-mood radar had gone off and they had scarpered. I could hear kid noises outside. I opened the window and stuck my head out. "Come inside I want to talk to you."

What's taking them so long? I fumed as I stirred the pile on the floor hoping to see my bag. Alas it was not there. My frustration rose as a search under both beds revealed nothing more than dirty socks and dust balls. I stuck my head around the side of the door and yelled, "hurry up."

The girls picked up their speed and dawdled into the room. Their hair was unbrushed and they were still in their

Wendy Hamilton

pajamas.

"When I tell you to clean up your room, I don't mean just stuff everything into the closet," I scolded, with my hands on my hips. "Rubbish…" I picked up a ball of paper and a broken truck, "goes in the rubbish bin. I want you to clean this up."

I stomped out of the room and into the kitchen. The hands of the clock on the wall had moved more than I expected.

Oh no we are going to be late for church again.

My search for the baby bag intensified. I squandered fifteen minutes looking for it in all the likely spots, ten minutes in all the unlikely ones and finally located it in the ridiculous place of the sandpit.

"I wish you kids would leave things alone," I yelled as I banged and brushed sand out of all the pockets and crevices of my sad looking bag.

I glared at the office door resentfully. It would be so good to be a man.

I filled up the gritty pockets with diapers and replaced the empty Baby-Wipes packet with a new one. Of course, all the little Tupperware containers for the raisins and crackers had disappeared. I bet they are in the toy box, I thought with a flash of insight. I stomped through to the girl's room. Not surprisingly, it was still a mess.

"Stop playing with your doll Marie and get on with cleaning up," I barked. She dropped it and trailed half-heartedly over to the pile on the floor. "You too Hannah, leave the cat alone."

I fossicked through the toys and unearthed my Tupperware containers. They were filled with hard play-dough and broken crayons.

"These are not for you to play with," I snapped as I left

I Told You Not To Climb The Cactus

the room. In the kitchen, I threw away the play-dough and washed everything in the sink. The clock informed me that another half hour had passed.

We were going to be *really* late this morning.

I stuffed snacks into the containers hastily and dropped them into the bag. The baby started bawling, cutting short my journey to the stroller.

"Not again," I groaned sniffing the air. I picked him up and he rewarded me by throwing-up all down my back. Now we both needed changing. Jealousy of the redwood door increased exponentially.

Hello, it would be nice to have some help, I fumed inwardly. *Yes, I know you are the church treasurer and you are working on the books but does it need to take ALL your spare time.* I mouthed it as I glared at the door but I did not say it. After all, good Christian wives do not say such belligerent things to their husbands, especially on Sunday morning.

At last the baby and I were clean again. I picked up the baby-bag and resumed my journey.

Mercifully, the big stroller with the tray on the bottom stood ready to go. I slung the replenished bag over the handle and dumped our Bibles in the tray. The girls (making the most of my preoccupation) had drifted out of their room. I waded through the pile of junk towards the closet.

Hmmm, I stared at the small pinafores hanging from the hangers. They can wear this and this, I thought, picking out two outfits. I laid one on each bed and rummaged through the chest of draws for tights and skivvies to go with them.

"Now where was the little stroller? Not folded up and hanging off the hook in the back entranceway where it should be, of course. The hum and rattle of wheels moving swiftly, caught my attention. If the ruckus outside was anything to go by, it was the chariot in a vigorous game.

Sometimes it stinks to be right.

"Get out of there Marie!" I bawled out the window. "How many times have I told you, you're too big to ride in the stroller? It is for the baby! You girls are being very naughty."

"Marie told me too," sniffed Hannah dissolving into tears.

"I don't care, is she your mother? Would you jump off a cliff if Marie told you to?" Like every other mother, I did not wait for an answer to the ancient question. "Get inside both of you and put on your church clothes."

I stomped outside and retrieved the small stroller. Miraculously, it still had four wheels. They bowed out but thankfully they still worked.

"Mummy, I can't find my clothes." Marie twirled on her tiptoes like a ballerina in low riding pajama pants.

By now we had less than ten minutes to get out the door.

"What do you mean you can't find them, I put them on your bed, have you *looked* on your bed?"

"I can't see them."

I stomped through to the bedroom.

"What do you think these are, Marie?" I hissed. "Open your eyes!"

At least Hannah had started to dress herself; difficulties were developing, however.

"Hannah your top is on back to front and inside out," I said correcting the problem.

"Ow, ow, you're pulling my head off," Hannah shrieked.

I thought of the clock on the wall as I helped her on with her tights and buttoned her pinafore. Finally, one of them

I Told You Not To Climb The Cactus

was ready to go. I turned around only to find that Marie (who theoretically could dress herself) was wandering about in her underclothes and playing with the cat. The baby started howling. His pants needed changing *again*. I was about to tear my hair out when the toddler came in. He was clutching a plant by its roots and covered with dirt.

That does it!

I marched through to the back bedroom and flung open the office door.

Ian looked up caught by surprise at the sight of the hostile, frazzled woman standing before him.

"I am so jealous of you," I spat out. "You get to sit here on the computer while I have to get the kids ready."

The baby was not the only one crying now. My husband got up and folded me in his arms.

"What do you want me to do?" he asked kindly.

"*You shouldn't need to even ask it is so obvious,*" I railed.

Ian was a young man who still had a lot to learn. He did, however, know how to do the most important thing. He held me tight and let me get all the anger and tears out.

"Why don't you sit down and have a nice cup of tea, while I change Joe and Mark," he said kindly.

"We don't have time, we will be late for church," I sniffed, rubbing my eyes.

"We are already late, a bit later won't matter," he answered soothingly.

I nodded and shuffled off to the kitchen, making sure not to look at the clock. As I sipped my tea and relaxed, I could hear Ian sorting out the kids. We were going to be late there was no doubt about it, but suddenly I did not care. My husband had listened to me and what is more, had taken action. I did not have to feel jealous of the redwood door

Wendy Hamilton

anymore; on Sunday mornings it stayed open. We still never made it to church on time, even with the two of us working together. But at least now I did not feel like Little Red Hen with all the work.

I Told You Not To Climb The Cactus

More Rest on Sunday.

It was very late indeed by the time we eventually got to the small church we regularly attended. The door ushers were long gone and most of the songs had been sung by the time we slunk in and parked the two strollers at the end of the pew.

Pastor Philip did not see us enter. He and his wife made a distinguished pair as they stood on the side of the stage. At forty-something, Kathleen was that rare type of woman who gets better looking as she ages. Philip, tall and dressed in a navy-blue suit, was clean-shaven with short curly hair. His dark sunglasses hid the fact he had no eyeballs.

I slid onto the seat and fished in the baby bag for the first Tupperware container, while Ian lifted Joe out of the stroller and sat him on the floor at our feet.

"Here you go," I whispered to Joe, handing him a plastic car and a small cracker to keep him quiet.

Wendy Hamilton

"I want my book," Marie's shrill voice piped up.

"Shhh," I said, passing her and Hannah a coloring-in-book each.

"Where are the crayons?"

"Here," I said passing a second Tupperware container down the row to her.

By now the sermon had started.

"Let us turn to Psalm 45," said Philip.

I reached down and pulled the Bibles from the tray under the big stroller. That was when I discovered Joe had loaded the tray with his soft toys when I was not looking.

The baby who had fallen asleep during the walk to church, stirred. I joggled the side of his pushchair and he drifted off again.

"Look at my picture," Hannah said in a stage whisper. She lifted up her book to display a yellow horse.

I put my finger to my lips, smiled and handed her and Marie a carrot stick. Joe started to grizzle and I cracked open another container hastily. The sermon finished as I eked out the last of the raisins.

After the service, we gathered in the back room for tea and cake.

Philip was a kid magnet. Marie and Hannah claimed a knee each and climbed onto him.

"Can I see your lost eyes Pastor Philip?" asked Marie. It was a favorite question with all the kids.

Philip took off his glasses and let them pry his eyelids open.

"Oooooooooooh!" The smooth pink membrane was marvelously impressive.

"Tell us again how you lost them? Marie said. She asked the same question every week and every week the answer

I Told You Not To Climb The Cactus

was different.

"Well one-day Snagglepuss, I went to the doctor. He was a mean man and he got a little teaspoon and dug them out." For a man of the cloth, Philip was surprisingly good at telling outrageous lies.

"Did it hurt very much?" asked Hannah sympathetically.

"Yes, very much Dumpling.

"Tell us a story Pastor Philip," commanded Marie.

"There once was a big giant called Goliath and a little boy called David," started Philip solemnly. His mouth twitched with mischief. If he had possessed eyes, they would have twinkled.

"No, not that one, tell us a Snagglepuss and Dumpling one."

"Alright, once upon a time there were two little girls called Snagglepuss and Dumpling. They were very bad little girls."

Marie and Hannah squirmed with delight.

Hannah took her thumb out of her mouth and looked at Philip solemnly. "It's a story about Marie and me," she said smiling.

"That's right Dumpling."

"Of course it is," said Marie jiggling impatiently. "What naughty things did we do?"

"These two girls were so naughty they got shut up in prison,"

More delight.

"And the only way they could get out was to flush themselves down the toilet where they ended up in the sewer floating in all the poohs and wees."

The girls were ecstatic. The story had surpassed their expectations.

Wendy Hamilton

"Those are rude words," said Hannah solemnly.

"Your mother will wash your mouth out with soap and water," said Marie delighted. "Tell us what happened next?"

"You don't really want to know," teased Philip.

"Yesssss, we do! Tell us, tell us pleeeeeeeease."

"Snagglepuss and Dumpling were so dirty that when they got home, their mother put them into the washing machine on the heavy-duty cycle." Philip paused.

"Then what happened?"

"She pinned them out on the clothesline to dry."

Quite the perfect ending.

"That story is even better than last week's one," said Hannah.

"What one was that?" asked Philip.

"The one where Snagglepuss and Dumpling were chopped up and made into meat pies for lions to eat," cut in Marie climbing down from Philip's knee. She rushed through the swing doors calling loudly to a small boy who was running around in the Sanctuary. "Hey David, listen to this. Once there were two girls called Snagglepuss and Dumpling." The rest of her words were cut off as the double doors flipped shut again.

I handed the storyteller a cup of tea and took one for myself. It was impossible to enjoy it, however. An unpleasant smell wafting about was ruining the flavor of my tea.

"What is that foul smell?" I asked Ian quietly.

"I think it is coming from over there," he replied pointing in the direction of our big stroller.

We walked towards it.

"It's definitely coming from this direction," I said sniffing like a bloodhound. "The smell seems to be coming from between Joe's soft toys on the tray."

I Told You Not To Climb The Cactus

I spied Marie and David hard at work

Wendy Hamilton

"*Aw yuck,*" said Ian hoisting a dirty diaper aloft.

"Oooo, that is ripe," I said horrified. "He must have raided the nappy-bin when I wasn't looking. How many are there?"

"Six," said Ian digging the offensive things out from under a pink elephant and two big teddy bears.

"Here give them to me, I'll get rid of them," I said taking them off Ian. I carried them into the Ladies Room and dumped them in the bin there. Through the open toilet door, I spied Marie and David hard at work. The inserts of many toilet rolls lay scattered around them while a great cloud of white tissue paper puffed out of the bowl. I was just in time to see them pull the flush-lever.

"*What are you doing?*" I shrieked as the water overflowed the toilet bowl and flooded onto the floor.

"We are sending it to prison," piped up my unquenchable child.

I rushed out and grabbed my husband.

"The kids have blocked the toilet!"

"Oh no, we don't want a plumbers bill!" As the church treasurer he was sensitive to unnecessary expenditure.

"Who, us or the church?"

"Neither," he said rushing into the Ladies Room.

For the next hour he worked feverishly to defuse the problem while David's mother and I lectured our offspring. Finally, the toilet was operational again.

We were the last to leave the church, just as well we had a key. Ian locked up while I strapped the toddler and the baby into their strollers.

"I'm hungry grizzled Hannah. Marie swinging on the metal handrailing, lost her grip and fell onto the graveled carpark. She let out a howl as the small stones grazed her

I Told You Not To Climb The Cactus

knees.

"It will be alright," I said dabbing the blood with my handkerchief. "It's not bleeding much. I'll find a plaster for it when we get home." I knew I should have gone through the whole kiss-it-better routine but I felt too exhausted to start. By now the baby and the toddler were bawling as well.

Ian and I took a stroller each.

"Hold onto the side of the pushchair," I said to Hannah wearily.

I turned to Ian as we started to trudge home, "so much for Sunday being a day of rest," I snorted.

Wendy Hamilton

Fiona and Friends.

"The next Fashion-Fiona I see lying around with no clothes on, goes in the rubbish," threatened my husband. He waved a curvy nudist in the air.

"Noooo, don't throw them out," squealed Marie and Hannah as they rushed about gathering up naked dolls.

"Why do they pull all the clothes off them and throw them around?" Ian asked me mystified.

I pondered on his question. "I think it is a brain development thing," I mused. "Perhaps it's like language. Remember how before the kids could speak, we used to say *where's Daddy, point to catty* and they would wave at you and point at the cat?"

"Yeah that was cute."

"I expect there is a brain lag between undressing and dressing dolls."

"A ten-year lag," growled Ian morosely. "This has been going on for a long time and I am sick of it."

"You could be right," I sighed.

I Told You Not To Climb The Cactus

"Marie and Hannah, I'm going outside and when I come back in, I will throw out all the naked dolls I find," Ian repeated his threat before stomping out.

The girls nodded mechanically. Already the frantic tidying had slowed to a halfhearted dawdle. They did not really believe their father would carry out his threat. I looked around in frustration. There were little bitty clothes scattered all over the floor. Ben (Fiona's boyfriend) lay decapitated, his head on Cinderella-Fiona's neck. Snow White Fiona still had her original head but her nylon hair had completely lost its shiny sleekness. It fuzzed around her face like a toilet brush. Model-Fiona did not have that problem. She had encountered a budding hairdresser. Her hair, cropped close to her head, bristled like a small stress relief ball. The idea of squeezing it did not, however, lower my tension. The boys also, were playing with Fiona dolls, but not the way the girls did.

"Stop hitting the cat with Fiona," I intervened.

As I moved swiftly to rescue the cat, I stood on a building block. "Ow, ow, ow," I yelped.

The agony of a small block in the arch of a barefoot has to be experienced to be believed. I sucked in my breath sharply and glared at the nine hundred and ninety-eight other building blocks lounging between the doll's clothes. I started picking them up, counting as I went because they were borrowed from the Toy Library.

"One, two, three, four….." It was a big job.

"Nine hundred and ninety-six,"

"Nine hundred and ninety-seven,"

"Nine hundred and ninety-eight…" I paused and scanned the room nervously. *Where was block nine hundred and ninety-nine?*

Wendy Hamilton

I checked the front of the box in panic. The black marker stated nine hundred and ninety-nine blocks emphatically. When I took them back, there would have to be *exactly* nine hundred and ninety-nine blocks or there would be a fine. The librarians were very inflexible about this…and yes, they definitely counted.

Dumb, Wendy, *dumb*, I said to myself as I recounted and counted yet again. Alas the missing piece remained elusive.

I wrenched open the window and stuck my head out. "Ian," I called out to him anxiously, "*I've lost a block!*"

"What are you getting all het up about? It's only a block," Ian replied reasonably.

"*Only a block!* You haven't met the woman in charge of the Toy Library," I shuddered. "Come and help me look."

"Oh alright," said Ian leaning his garden fork against the fence before coming in.

We searched frantically under the couch, on the coffee table and in the toddler's mouth.

"What were you *thinking,* borrowing something that had nine-hundred and ninety-nine pieces?" Ian chided me.

"I have no idea. Thank goodness I never got the ten-thousand-piece jigsaw puzzle!"

"That car is the sort of thing you should stick to from now on," he said, referring to a huge peddle car parked by the fireplace. "It's too big to lose and too expensive to own."

"Way too expensive," I agreed. "Especially as the kids will have lost interest in it by the time it's due back."

"A two-week attention span, that sounds about right," said Ian groping behind the firewood basket.

"Soft toys are also a waste of time to get out," I said pulling the cushions off the couch in my search. "Apart from a couple of old worn-out favorites, they never play with the

I Told You Not To Climb The Cactus

hordes they've already got. No point importing any more. The only time they show any interest in them is when I suggest getting rid of some."

Blast that block, where could it be? I was almost at the point of despair when I spied it under the hall-table.

"There you are," I yelled, leaping on it as if it were a mouse about to get away. I dropped it in its big plastic container and snapped the clips shut.

"Thank goodness for that," said Ian going outside to the garden again.

"No more playing with the blocks," I informed the kids. "They are going back to the Toy Library tomorrow. Nine-hundred-and-ninety-nine pieces of anything is too stressful." I carried them through to my room and shut them away in the closet for safekeeping. On my way back I passed the girl's room. I glanced in and felt depressed.

The lid of the toy box sat up at an ugly angle, its open mouth was gorged on an excess of junk. Matchbox cars with missing wheels, tacky fast-food-toys, and Teddy Bears spewed out. A baby doll's bald head was covered in crayon graffiti and most of the coloring books had covers and pages missing. In addition, there was a lone dress-up-shoe (with a broken heel) jumbo blocks, and a clown with a floppy neck.

Sniff, sniff, what was that dreadful smell? It burned the back of my nose painfully. I dug deep into the pile and pulled out the offender; a Little-Miss.-make-up-kit. The lipstick had been eaten long ago but the scent bottle (even empty and rinsed out twice) retained its potency.

How much of this stuff actually had value?

I remembered my mother saying, "don't give kids things too soon and don't give them too much."

She was right. If I was writing a Dear Abby Column,

Wendy Hamilton

I would strongly suggest never giving tiny blocks or the controversial fashion doll's (if you have any intention of giving them at all) before age ten. And tell Grandma to save fluffy dice and soft toys for teenage boys. They like them as car decorations and presents for their girlfriends.

As I was not writing a column, however, I did something better. I got out a big black rubbish bag. While the kids were throwing Fiona's and cars around in the lounge, I sneakily raided the toy-box. I filled the first bag with soft toys and put it aside for the Salvation Army. The Little-Miss-make-up-kit and everything broken went into a second bag ready for the rubbish collection.

"What are you doing with all those toys Mum?" Marie swung on the handle of her bedroom door.

I jumped guiltily. She had not seen the rubbish bags yet because I had cunningly positioned them out of sight.

"I'm tidying up and if you come in here, I will give you a job," I said. In this situation attack was the best form of defense. The threat worked like a treat. There was a rush of wind as the door slammed behind Marie's fleeing figure.

"Hmm," I thought, surveying the remaining toys. I could make my own toy library. When my boys were really ready for the tiny building blocks, I would buy my own. Moreover, I would be very flexible about the number of pieces returned to the box. Meanwhile, these jumbo blocks were just perfect for my toddler's development. I threw them into a plastic box and snapped on the lid. I made zip-top packs of coloring books and crayons. Next, I scrubbed the baby doll's head clean and sewed non-removable clothes onto her cloth body. I sorted and washed the dress-up clothes, added a few new exciting hats and skirts and stored them all away in a special suitcase. I gathered all the fast-food toys into a pillowcase

I Told You Not To Climb The Cactus

and renamed them 'The sicky Toys' with the conditional note attached, 'use only in convalescence.'

Now where could I store my Toy Library? Not in the old toy box. I wandered about the house speculatively. My eye fell on a huge divan with an upholstered lid. Just the thing; into this, I neatly stowed all my tidy boxes and bags of sorted toys and activities.

When I was finished, I called the kids. They came reluctantly, expecting to get a job.

"This is Mummy's toy box." They stared at it curiously, happy that it was not a chore. "Nobody is to touch Mummy's box," I admonished. "This is where the special toys live. On wet days and afternoon quiet times, you get to choose two toys each."

They looked at me and bounced with excitement.

"You can all choose one toy now as a special treat."

They all chose carefully.

Marie took her coloring book and crayons.

Hannah took her baby doll.

Joe took his jumbo blocks.

Mark took his pull along duck.

For the next hour they played quietly, thrilled with their 'new' toys that they had thrown around the room hundreds of times before.

Meanwhile, secretively behind the closed door of the lounge, I stuffed all the naked Fiona's into a black plastic bag. While I worked, I thought about what kind of toys my kids really needed. A sandpit, bucket, and spade, a paddling pool, bikes, a trampoline, a small table and chair set, play dough, big old cardboard boxes (for building huts) and a swing. I already had a pot cupboard, trees, and a dirt pile.

By the end of the morning, my house felt tidy and

orderly. The toy box lid closed easily. Moreover, the closet door could be opened without risk of death-by-avalanche.

My mother knew a thing or two. When it comes to toys, less is definitely more!

I Told You Not To Climb The Cactus

The Teachable Moment.

Red-haired people have the reputation of having a hot temper. Whether humans deserve the accusation or not, ginger cats do.

We were in between cats. Our previous cat Oliver, was a gray tabby and a true gentleman. He was huge, elderly and extremely good natured.

"I've only heard him growl once," said my neighbor over the right-fence. "It was after my two-year-old had scooted his bike over his tail a few times."

Even in death, Oliver was considerate. One day I noticed he looked a bit frail and the next day he was gone.

"I didn't think he was looking too good yesterday, cats often go off to die," said Pearl when I consulted her over the left-fence. Pearl shared him with us. She was not a cat lover but Oliver (who acknowledged only cat boundaries) had won her over. He penetrated her heart to the extent she cooked him an egg laced with cream regularly. He had missed breakfast at our house, had not turned up for his egg at her house, and was not in his usual sunny spot.

Ian and I hunted for him but we never found his body.

When you get a special animal, they are hard to replace.

"If we ever get another cat, he must be a gray tabby," I said sadly.

A few days later the phone rang.

"The boss has found two kittens abandoned by the dumpster. Do you want one Wend?" asked Ian. "One of them is a tabby but it is not gray."

"What color is it?" I asked. "I thought they only came in gray.

"Ginger."

"That's right, tabbies *do* come in ginger. A marmalade-tabby. Hmm. I suppose it doesn't really matter. I think it is the stripes that make them so friendly, not the color."

"Yeah, I suppose," agreed Ian.

"Besides, auburn fur would go nicely with the red-brown tones of the floor," I said speculatively. I kept looking at the glowing wood with satisfaction as Ian and I deliberated over the phone. After years of waiting, the old carpet and vinyl were finally gone and the lovely timber floor exposed. The novelty of it and the pungent smell of polyurethane had not yet worn off.

"Yeah," agreed Ian humoring me. He did not care either way.

"Auburn would also look great on my big cream and brown mat," I added, looking at the Persian rug laid out in front of the black wood-range. "A cat is such a homely thing to have around. They really enhance country décor."

"Hmm, yeah, I suppose." We had been married long

I Told You Not To Climb The Cactus

enough for him to think this was a normal conversation.

I pushed the runner of a nearby rocking chair with my foot and watched it move back and forth. The gingham cushion on the seat looked empty. I sighed.

"What are patchwork quilts, cane baskets, freshly baked bread, and dried lavender, without a lazy cat curled up on a rocking chair?" I said.

"Is that a yes?" asked Ian tentatively.

"Bring him home," I said decisively.

The cardboard box was somewhat banged up by the time the kitten got home. That should have been a tip-off, but I glossed over it in the excitement of the unveiling. The four kids and I crowded around as Ian lifted the hyperactive little live-wire out. Released from his prison he rewarded his deliverer by sinking his needle teeth into the ball of Ian's thumb. Meanwhile his four little feet (fully extended into prickly fans) raked the air. He was stripy, but he did not look comfortable, homely or lazy. He was orange and very, very feisty.

"He will settle down when we get him neutered," I said. And as I had never had an orange cat before, I really believed it!

At first, we called him Harold-Wilson, the combined names of the kid's two grandfathers. It was a good big solid respectable name and the Grandfathers were flattered. I hoped it would encourage the kitten to grow into a good big solid respectable family member; just like Oliver and the grandfathers. Instead, he remained streamlined, feisty and hot-tempered.

"I don't think Harold-Wilson is a good fit for that cat," I said morosely, as I reached up and pulled him off my velvet curtains. He bit me as I put him on the floor.

Wendy Hamilton

"No," agreed Ian, sticking a plaster over a scratch on his hand (another gift from the cat.) He's a proper dumbo.

"*Dumbo*, now *that* is a suitable name," I said, rechristening him on the spot.

Dumbo ran everywhere, chased balls like a dog and never once sat cozily on anyone's knee. He scratched the legs of the rocking chair and shed orange hairs on my Persian rugs. Furthermore, he lay in ambush under beds; darting out in attack mode whenever a pair of unsuspecting legs passed by. He did not add restful ambiance to the country kitchen, he did not enhance the décor. Moreover, the puddles he left on my lovely timber floor powerfully eclipsed the scented vanilla candle.

The kids had fun with him but he was the only cat I never liked. Therefore, it was pure hypocrisy to be upset when he expired.

"Why am I crying?" I asked Ian on the morning he found him dead on the road. "I never liked that cat?"

The kids and I clustered around the small body that Ian had tastefully wrapped in a black rubbish-sack.

"Because it is sad," said Ian wiping his eyes surreptitiously. "I've dug a hole in the garden." As the man of the house he was automatically the undertaker and funeral director.

"Can I pick some flowers for his grave," sniffed Marie.

"Of course," said Ian putting his arm around her shoulder.

We all trooped outside and stood around the hole under the oak tree.

There were many genuine tears from the kids and a few crocodile ones from me, as we laid Dumbo to rest.

"I will miss him," said Hannah, looking fondly at all the scratches on her arms and legs.

I Told You Not To Climb The Cactus

"Get another kitten today," whispered Ian. "It will help them get over it." He kissed me goodbye and went off to work.

"How about we go to the pet shop and get a kitten," I said brightly at breakfast.

"A kitten!" The kids were excited; their grief was easily distracted by the magical word.

Now is my chance to get a gray tabby, I thought. I will not be making the mistake of getting another orange one. We cleaned the house hurriedly and scrambled into the van.

"Where do cat's go when they die?" asked Joe as I pulled out into a gap in the traffic.

"Don't you know anything?" said Marie. "They go to cat heaven."

"Is that right Mum?"

"Yes." I said it with more certainty than I actually felt. I had never been able to find a conclusive answer in the Bible to that one. There was nothing to say, however, that they did not.

"Do people die?" asked Mark pulling his thumb out of his mouth. Death was a new concept for the three-year-old.

"Yes, people die too."

"Grandma and Granddad will die soon, they're old," said Hannah solemnly.

"I think they have a wee way to go yet," I said. "They are still in their fifties."

"Sometimes, children die," said Marie. "That little boy at church died and he was only four."

"Yes, even children die sometimes," I admitted.

"Do people go to cat heaven?"

"No, they go to people heaven," said Marie.

"How do you get there?" asked Joe.

Wendy Hamilton

For the rest of the journey I got the chance to explain in simple language a great theological truth to my children. Because of Dumbo they listened attentively.

When we got downtown, I parked the van and we spent the whole morning trailing around the pet shops. There were kittens galore, but among them were no gray tabbies. To go home empty-handed was not an option.

"What about this one Mum?" said Hannah pointing to a sleek little jet-black one.

"Hmmm," I said unsure. "I did not want a repeat of Dumbo.

"She's got a tiny white spot on her chest," observed Marie.

"You had a black and white cat when you were a girl, didn't you?" said Joe remembering the stories I had told them.

"Blackie was a wonderful cat," I mused thoughtfully.

"Do you like her Mark?" I asked my youngest child.

"Yeah," said Mark poking his chubby finger through the cage and stroking the kitten. Small purrs vibrated the little body. Just then a beam of sunlight fell across her.

"Look at that," I said pointing to faint stripes in her pelt. "I think she must have a bit of tabby in her somewhere."

The decision was unanimous. We called her Molly and took her home consoled. As cats do not need companions, we did not need to buy another cat. In fact, I had no intention of ever owning two cats, but when a pet shop called a couple of days later and asked if we were still wanted a gray tabby, I caved. Morris was a couple of weeks younger than Molly and quite a bit smaller, a definite disadvantage in conflict. My initial thrill over a gray tabby was quickly replaced with other emotions as the kids went wild with excitement.

I Told You Not To Climb The Cactus

"Give him to me,"
"No, I want him."
"You're hogging him.
"Am not."
"Yes, you are."
"Well you had Molly."
The voices were escalating in noise and intensity.
"I like Morris better."
"So do I."
"*Don't say that in front of Molly,*" shouted Hannah (my most compassionate child) "*she'll hear you.*"
"*Cat's don't understand English, you donkey,*" yelled Joe (my least compassionate child.)
"*Stop it and leave the cat's alone!*" Now I was shouting.

The kids were driving me crazy as they fought with each other. The kittens also fought. Every time Molly came within striking distance of Morris, she would smack him hard on the head with a front paw. I spent my whole day separating fighting kids and fighting cats.

I could not even send them all outside as the rain had set in; great heavy soaking rain. Deep puddles spread over the back yard. Worse by far, were the pungent cat-puddles under the beds inside. By mid-afternoon, I had a meltdown.

"I want all you kids in separate rooms." I yelled. "Marie and Joe choose an activity and go to your bedrooms. Mark, you can play with the blocks in the lounge."

There was a general grumbling as Marie, Joe, and Mark drifted into different rooms.

I needed somewhere to put Hannah but I was running out of space. I wanted the kitchen and my bedroom for myself. Suddenly I had an inspiration.

"Hannah you can have the kittens." An undercurrent of

murmuring and a few whispers of "that's not fair," floated about. I ignored the comments and carried on. "I want you in the bathroom and take a rolled-up newspaper with you. Every time Molly smacks Morris rescue him and tap her with the newspaper."

"OK Mum," said Hannah pleased. She scooped up the kittens and marched off to the bathroom.

I went and lay down. My head pounded and my cup of tea was not the only thing in the room steaming. I never liked Dumbo, but if he had not got himself squashed on the road, I wouldn't be going through all this. Even in death, he was not a considerate gentleman. I could hear scuffling and banging coming from the bathroom. Hannah did not need an afternoon activity. She was preoccupied with umpiring the cats. A peculiar smell wafted up from under my bed. Gray tabby or not, I was seriously wondering about the wisdom of getting kittens.

The phone rang,

"How's it going Wend, how are the kittens getting on?" asked Ian.

"Horrible," I wailed "I wish we had never got them."

"What about the kids, are they still upset about Dumbo?"

"No, they are too excited over the replacements. They think two for one is a good deal."

"It might be a pain Wend, but it is better the kids first encounter with death is with a cat. Grandparents are not so easily replaced."

I pondered over the truth of Ian's words and remembered the great conversation I had had with the kids in the van. Dumbo's death created a teachable moment for me to pass on some of the weightier concepts about life and faith.

"You are right," I smiled. "Tomorrow we will make him

I Told You Not To Climb The Cactus

a tombstone."

In the back garden, there is a small wooden plaque, it reads,

Dumbo
In life he was useless,
But in death,
He was invaluable.

Wendy Hamilton

Life and Death.

Back in the bad old days when my mother was a child and everything was institutionalized, death was tidied up and swept away as quickly as possible.

Nana, who came from house-proud Scottish descent, cleaned it up excessively. Perhaps she thought the recognition of death would mark her wallpaper or leave mud on her kitchen floor. More likely she had not yet made peace with her maker, and wished to hide our inevitable fate from herself. Whatever the reasoning, my mother was diligently shielded from funerals. Death and cemeteries were shrouded in a deep cloak of mystery and it was not until she was newly married she faced her first funeral. In keeping with her training, Mum had no intention of going. My father, however, was not having a bit of it.

"Of course, you are going!"

"I am not!" Mum was tearfully adamant.

"Don't be ridiculous." Dad was equally adamant.

"I've never been to a funeral before."

I Told You Not To Climb The Cactus

"You're kidding?"

"No, Mum always shielded us from funerals."

"Well, it is high time you went." He was unsympathetic.

"I couldn't." Mum was shaking at the idea.

"She was my auntie and you will come with me!"

According to my mother, Dad almost had to carry her into the church she was so petrified.

Once seated, however, things changed. Mum, who views death merely as a door to a better world, was charmed with the whole ceremony. From that day on she saw funerals as huge social events and took us to them from a young age. Us kids liked them because the deceased was some old person we did not know very well and there were lots of cream cakes afterward. Sometimes I cried but only because I felt sorry for the people around me who looked upset. Even the death of my grandparents brushed over me lightly, as they lived a long way off and we seldom saw them. I was about nine when my grandfather died; and even then, I was more staggered by the concept of death rather than any real sense of loss.

At nearly forty Ian still had all his grandparents alive. The family had an explanation for the longevity.

"It's all that whole-meal flour and righteous living," said Elizabeth.

Ian's maternal grandfather was the first to go. (That side of the family ate less whole-meal scones.) We flew down to Tauranga and of course took the children.

"There is a viewing of the body for the family tomorrow morning if you kids want to go," said my mother-in-law. "Dad and I have already been."

I had attended many funerals but I had never actually seen a dead body. I felt curiosity arise in me as Ian's brother, two sisters and our family filed around the open coffin. Granddad lay still, but he did not look asleep. He looked like one of the waxworks at the Gum-diggers Museum. Even those wax figures gave me an eerie feeling. They were so lifelike but the intangible spirit was disturbingly absent.

Granddad had definitely gone. We stood in awe around the rim of the coffin and stared at his earthly shell solemnly. It is hard to keep up solemn awe for long. Rubella, shedding it first, gently felt her grandfather's finger.

"It feels cold like fresh chicken from the supermarket."

This observation was tremendously interesting. David and Elizabeth also made experimental pokes and prods at the neatly folded hands. But I kept my fingers well away.

"Someone has put cigarettes in Granddad's pocket," said Rubella gently pulling out three hand-rolled cigarettes.

We all smiled as she tucked them back in, it seemed so right. "I'm glad he's wearing a plaid shirt," said Elizabeth stroking the red and black flannel shirt.

"So *him*," I agreed. "A suit would seem strange."

"I wonder if he is dressed under the satin blanket?" mused Rubella.

We discussed the question at length but nobody was disrespectful enough to even *think* of looking.

"The coffin is lovely timber. Do you think it is walnut or mahogany?" asked Ian.

"Too dark for walnut," I said firmly.

"There is a gap between the satin liner and the coffin," observed David. "Can you rent a coffin?"

There was a lively debate for and against the possibility. One thing was sure, it could definitely be done. If you felt carefully, you could feel there was actually a box within a box. All this close investigation around the rim of the coffin

I Told You Not To Climb The Cactus

led to another discovery. Four-year-old Hannah was just the right height for her mouth to be in line with the edge of the casket.

"Hannah has chewed along the edge and I can see her teeth marks!" I said appalled.

There was a general rush around to our side as everyone looked to see how deep they were.

"They won't come out" said Elizabeth rubbing a tissue back and forth briskly. "They are quite deep."

"Don't worry," said David calmly, "they won't show when the lid is screwed on."

As six-year-old Marie was swinging off one of the pallbearers handles, we decided to leave before there was a big distressing accident.

At the church, Hannah's teeth marks and Ian's wax grandfather were neatly hidden. Instead, we focused on the magnificent bouquet of lilies that spread across the lid. As the preacher concluded the service and the casket was lowered out of sight, I was grateful for the morning's experience. Somehow, all the irreverent arguing, talk of supermarket chicken and Hannah's childish gnawing, clawed death back into life. My mother was right, death was just a doorway into another world. What mattered was making your peace with God before you went to meet him. The hard thing is the loss of a person, not death itself.

I turned to my husband as we sat on the plane on our way home.

"I am glad you come from a line of long-livers. I will go before you."

He turned to me and I waited for him to say something loving about me.

"Not the way I drive!" he said mischievously.

Wendy Hamilton

Four is Quite Enough!

It was one of those days. The house oozed kids. Marie was continually in my space, talking and asking stupid questions just for the sake of hearing her own voice. There was a lot of noise and movement going on up and down the hallway. It was Hannah taking her little 'doggies' for a walk.

"Hurry up doggies," commanded Hannah.

Joe and Mark obediently trotted a bit faster as she tugged the string leash tied around their tummies.

"Now go outside. Joe, pretend you are eating dog food and Mark can be the baby," she added.

I heard a lot of banging and thumping as the little mother threw all the toys out of the cane doll's pram and humped it down the veranda steps. I thought about calling her back to clean up all the mess she had just made, but the idea of her going outside was too pleasant to interfere with. The pram had belonged to my mother's sister when she was

I Told You Not To Climb The Cactus

a child and passed down to me. It was at least forty years old, heavy, and substantial compared to modern toys. It had been repainted multiple times and had seen many strangely dressed chickens and cats ride in its depths. At a very low point of its history, it had been a credible go-cart. The hood still wore a souvenir from that time, a small broken piece of cane, big enough to poke a finger through. Apart from that, it was still in good condition. It even had its original solid rubber tires.

Hannah lifted the heavy two-year-old with difficulty and dumped him in. He sat opposite the hood with his feet on the pillow and sucked his finger happily.

"Come on Doggie," she called to Joe, "you can stop eating now. We will go for a walk to the shops."

She tied his lead onto the side of the pram's handle and trundled her cumbersome load along the path around the house. She stopped to buy fruit at the lemon tree, vegetables at the nasturtium bush, and candy at the monkey apple tree. By the time she got 'home,' again, her red handbag was bulging.

"Now we will have dinner. You can be a boy again Joe," she said untying him and dumping Mark on the ground. The boys sat happily munching on sour lemons and monkey apples. They are very obedient for her, I thought enviously. Perhaps I should get her to teach them how to dust the hall table. It was a foolish thought. Nobody would want to play at something I wanted to be done.

"Don't forget to eat your greens?" said the boy's pseudo-mother as she cut the peppery leaves with a stick and handed bits to them. If I had dished up lemons, monkey apples and nasturtium leaves, and told them to eat them up, they would have fussed like anything.

Wendy Hamilton

"Sit down over here and I will read you a story."

She gathered the boys on either side of her and read The Cat and the Hat to them. The verbal words did not always match the right page and her memory failed her at a couple of points. But her ad-libs were just as satisfactory to her audience as the printed story, so it did not matter in the least.

Despite feeling overrun with kids like the old woman in the shoe, there was an advantage of having more than one child. I did not have to be a playmate. Years ago, I saw a neighbor playing in the garden with her only child. I remember thinking, if I ever have children, I would want more than one. I would HATE to have to be a playmate. I would not have the attention span for it. Besides, nobody excels at playing like kids do, and even sibling fights (as frequent and irritating as they are) serve a purpose. No child can maintain the illusion he is the center of the world if he has siblings. Even if he still believes in his heart that he is a supreme being, the idea will be hotly contested every day.

It had gone quiet in the garden. I peeped out the door and saw something really sweet. Hannah was leading her small brothers in a prayer meeting. I could hear her intensely petitioning The Almighty about something and tuned in.

"Please God could you send Mummy another baby for us to play with."

I suddenly went cold and looked up towards heaven in terror. Kid's prayers were powerful because they prayed with so much faith. I remembered the cat of my childhood. He lived for twenty-one years because my sisters and I prayed extensions on his life. And my poor mother hadn't wanted a kitten in the first place!

"Please, please, please cancel that request Lord, I beseech you don't listen.

I Told You Not To Climb The Cactus

Hannah takes her doggies for a walk.

Wendy Hamilton

We do not want any more children in this house. Four is quite enough!"

I marched out briskly hoping to break up the application process before the petition lodged in the 'To Do' basket of God's filing system. How often, I wondered nervously, had Hannah prayed that prayer?

"Stop that Hannah and come in," I called tensely.

"I want lunch over early. I need the whole afternoon to talk to God about something urgently!"

I Told You Not To Climb The Cactus

Time out.

I stretched back in the comfortable reclining chair and flexed my feet in pleasurable relaxation. The luxury was expensive but worth every cent. I had a precious hour with no interruptions, no arguments over toys and no teaching Mark to be nice to the cat. Furthermore, there were no sticky fingerprints on the wall and only adult conversation flowed into my ears. The deep tones of fully-grown voice boxes sounded mellow and soothing.

I closed my eyes and thought contentedly of the blue and orange fish with the long filmy tails swimming about in the next room. Nobody was trying to catch them with a tea-strainer, they swam about unmolested. I opened my mouth and a low drone overshadowed the pleasant flute music. You know you are a seasoned mother when going to the dentist is a recreational highlight.

"The hardest thing about being a full-time mother is being on call twenty-four seven with no breaks," I complained to Ian when he came looking for me after work one day. "I've

Wendy Hamilton

been counting down the minutes until you come home."

I sat slumped on the veranda. The thickness of the front door was the only thing between me and my clamoring offspring. Their misty outlines behind me, peeped through the frosted glass. Mercifully, the door toned down the constant noise of shrill voices.

"I feel like the Tavinor's Alsatian when it had pups," I wailed, remembering a childhood incident. "It ran around a large hole until all ten puppies fell in. We thought it was hilarious how Sheba peered down at the squiggling mass trying to climb up the sides. Now I know *exactly* how that dog felt and it is not funny at all," I finished darkly.

"Has it been a bad day?" asked Ian, sliding down the door to sit beside me.

"Bad does not do it justice," I said bitterly. "So bad I could be tempted to go to a Ladies Camp, provided there are no kids there and they cook all my meals."

"That bad, huh," said my husband. He did not like ladies camps either, but for an entirely different reason. He got to be the primary caregiver for the duration of the camp.

"Why don't you go for a nice walk by yourself and I will deal with the kids," he suggested kindly.

"That would be nice," I sniffed weakly. He got up and went around to the back of the house. I stayed seated until I heard the delighted screams of "*Dad's home*" and heard many feet thunder off towards the kitchen. I opened the door cautiously and whisked into our bedroom for my purse. I froze as the horribly all too familiar sound of, "Mum, Mum," floated down the hallway.

"Come back here and leave your mother alone," Ian called Marie back. "Mum just needs a bit of time out. How would you kids like spaghetti for dinner?"

I Told You Not To Climb The Cactus

I could hear a ruckus of approval as I slipped out the door. My tired body drifted up the path and out the front gate. Ohhh, the bliss of moving alone. No pushchair, no distracted children wandering onto the road, and nobody talking my ears off. The mere novelty of it gave wings to my feet. I sped along the footpath and whisked across roads like an escaped prisoner.

The corner dairy in the distance arrested my attention. A sandwich-board outside the door displayed the image of an ice cream; a chocolate-dipped, caramel centered ice cream. Moreover, it was floating in a tropical paradise under the words *Get One Today*. The command was entirely reasonable and I obeyed with alacrity. My pace slowed to a meander as I leisurely licked. While the ice cream could not transport me to paradise, the lack of children did. I sucked the last creamy drop off the stick and dropped it into a rubbish bin at a nearby park. My speed picked up again as the sugar rush hit and I strode briskly along the street until a voice halted me.

"Hello, Wendy," said the voice. It was Sue, a friend from church. She had a preschooler in tow and was pushing a stroller.

"Hello, Sue, nice to see you," I said. "How have you been?"

"Tired, I wish I had your energy," she answered candidly.

"My energy," I snorted. "What you're looking at is a snippet of energy in a big desert of exhaustion."

"Oh Wendy, you make me laugh," she said smiling with disbelief.

There was no point arguing with her. I eyed the fussy toddler in her stroller and cringed. The last thing I wanted was to snail home at the pace of someone else's child.

Wendy Hamilton

"Sorry I can't stop I've got to get home. I'll catch up with you on Sunday," I apologized.

"Yes, that would be good, see you then," she said as I zoomed off.

I loitered about the streets looking at interesting houses. On a street, by the railway line, I discovered a peach tree. It was self-seeded and growing in no-man's-land by the side of the tracks. Even better, it was dripping with ripe fruit. I stayed there gorging on peaches until the street lamps switched on. The lamps were the sign that my wonderful husband would have the kids fed and in bed.

"How was that?" asked Ian as I slipped in the back door quietly. He looked like the last few hours had knocked the stuffing out of him.

"Wonderful, it was so nice to be by myself for a change." I loaded my plate with leftover spaghetti while Ian made me a cup of tea.

"Why do people look at me and get the erroneous idea that I am a person with abundant energy?" I asked him as I sat down at the table.

"Beats me," said Ian who knew the daily reality.

"One good thing did happen today," (my short reprieve had given me a better perspective of the day,) "I bought a new vacuum cleaner," I said, twirling long strings of spaghetti around my fork.

"About time," said Ian. "The hose keeps falling off that old thing in the cupboard."

"The best part is it was on special and has a reusable dust-bag."

"That will be a saving," approved Ian, thinking of all the money we had spent on disposable bags over the years. "Have you tried it out yet?"

I Told You Not To Climb The Cactus

"No, the day spun out of control when I got home."

"Where is it?" Ian was keen to try it out. Anything connected with technology fascinated him, even a new vacuum cleaner.

"Not now," I said alarmed. "You will wake up the kids, I'll try it out tomorrow."

Tomorrow rolled around quickly. I zoomed through the housework for the treat of cleaning the floor. The sight of toast crumbs and peas lying under the kitchen table made me unusually happy.

"Let's try this little sucker out," I said to a doomed spider on the ceiling as I pulled my new toy out of its box. It was bright yellow, lightweight, and made in China.

I pulled the long cord out of its nifty inner-sprung holder and plugged it in. The suck was gratifyingly fierce as I energetically whisked around the lounge. The spare set of car keys (lost under the couch) zoomed up the hose with rattling good zest. The kitchen was done almost as quickly. The crumbs, peas, a stray meatball, and two coins disappeared without trouble. Things started to slow down around the cat's bowl. I had to take the broad end-attachment off to suck up the kitty-biscuits. I kept the end off for the hallway and scrubbed backward and forwards at the dust balls gathered at the foot of the skirting board. Something was not quite right. I tested the hose with the palm of my hand. It made a squeaking noise and the suction felt weaker than when I started. I was satisfied, however, that there was still some life in it. It was in the bedroom that the rot set in. The suction dropped alarmingly.

"This is ridiculous," I said aloud, as I picked hair and cotton bits off the floor and poked them into the hose. It was a hopeless situation, but I persisted until the overload switch popped out. I looked at my yellow bargain lying comatose on the floor. It was the same shape and color as the one on the infomercial but its performance was infinitely inferior. The one on the TV could suck up sixteen tennis balls and still lift a bag of cement out of the carpet. I was not sure how many tennis balls, six peas, a meatball, two coins, a few dust-balls, and a handful of kitty-biscuits were equivalent to. I knew, however, that it was a lot less than sixteen. Furthermore, any cement dust would remain firmly embedded in the carpet.

It was several hours before my new toy was sufficiently rested to start again. Despite its deceptive appearance of efficiency, my bargain was not as robust as my mother's old 1960s vacuum cleaner. The 1960s model was three times the weight and ten times uglier than the slick new one. It could, however, work all day and the hose never twisted or jackknifed (another problem I had encountered.)

By the afternoon my vacuum cleaner was not the only one overloaded. I lay on the couch with my energy source unplugged. The house was blissfully bathed in a suspicious not-golden-silence. I, however, foolishly lapped it up. In my permanently sleep-deprived state, it did not take much to drift off into dreamland. I was rudely awakened a few hours later by the toddler hitting me on the head with a wooden bus.

"Ow," I shrieked jerking up. Mark grinned at me as if he had done something clever. "What is that all over your face?" I said looking at him through bleary eyes.

"Mark, good boy," babbled Mark happily.

I focused and saw that someone had indeed rewarded him for good behavior. His whole face was covered with small smiley faces.

"Who's been into the schoolwork cupboard and taken

I Told You Not To Climb The Cactus

my smiley stamp?" I yelled leaping up. There was no answer, the house was empty. I stomped through the kitchen and was about to go outside when something caught my eye. It was a small pile of gray and brown fluff. "That vacuum cleaner is worse than I realized," I said to the spider who had escaped it. I stooped down and poked at the mound. It was soft, familiar, and not the fault of the vacuum cleaner. An awful suspicion entered my mind, that grew when I saw a pair of discarded scissors lying nearby.

"Have you kids been playing hairdressers again?" I bawled out the door.

No answer. I could hear stage whispers in the garage, however.

I strode down the garden path towards the garage, collecting more shocks every step.

"I've told you kids, not to weed the garden without an adult with you," I fumed, looking at marigold seedlings lying with their roots exposed on the path. "And leave Daddy's tools alone." By now I had reached the garage. I poked my head around the door. "What are you doing in here?" I asked.

"Nothing," chorused three voices.

"I don't call this nothing," I growled pointing at Hannah and the cat. Hannah's fringe had been cropped back to the roots while the cat looked like a mangy poodle. "I've told you before Marie, you're not to cut hair."

"It wasn't me," said Marie self-righteously. "It was Hannah and I told her not to," she finished smugly.

"*You did not,*" shouted Hannah.

"Yes, I did."

"That was very naughty Hannah," I hissed. I turned back to Miss. Smug.

"Were you the one who took my smiley-face stamp out

of the cupboard?" I asked.

The smug look disappeared and she looked at her feet.

I took the change in body language to mean *yes*.

"That was very naughty, you know you are not to touch that stamp. It is only for very good behavior and nice schoolwork."

Marie lifted her head and looked me in the eye. "Mark *was* good and we were playing schools," she said in self-justification.

"Don't try to squirm out of it young lady," I snapped, pointing my finger at her.

"I made you some perfume." Joe interrupted me by handing me a honey pot. I looked at the crushed roses floating about in the water. He had me on the horns of a dilemma. Did I thank him for his gift or blast him for raiding my rose bushes?

"Go to your rooms," I said, doing neither.

They scarpered keen to escape my gimlet eye. I meanwhile, replaced Ian's tools in the toolkit and replanted the marigolds.

By the time I got back inside my mood was volatile. It was exceedingly unfortunate, that the Religious-Tract-Visitors arrived at my door the exact moment that I discovered a heap of grass clippings in the entranceway. It was even more unfortunate that the door was open. I do not know who was more embarrassed by the horrible noise that erupted from my mouth.

Shame! I have deteriorated into a screaming mother I thought miserably, as the man and woman shot back down the pathway. I slumped into an armchair and stared listlessly at the tree out the window. How had things got to this state? What happened to the quiet afternoons I used to have

I Told You Not To Climb The Cactus

when the girls were small? Back then I insisted Marie and Hannah stayed in their rooms for two hours after lunch. Like many great routines, it had slid away. Home-schooling had compounded the problem.

"If the girls went to school like other kids, I would get a break from them every day," I complained to Ian later that evening.

"Do you want to stop home-schooling them?" he asked.

"No, I just need to carve out some me-time. Remember how I used to make the girls stay in their rooms for two hours after lunch?"

"Yeah, you used to let them choose something out of the toy box and an activity."

"That's right. Story tapes and coloring in books and stuff. I'm thinking to do that again. The boys can choose from the toy box and the girls can do art."

"It will only work if they are all in separate rooms," cautioned Ian.

"Don't I know it," I grimaced ruefully. "I don't want to spend my precious two hours arbitrating fights. I would rather cross-stitch or read a book if I have the energy."

"You should do it," said Ian.

"I will," I said decisively.

I implemented my plan the next day. As it had in earlier years, it worked a treat.

"How did the afternoon quiet time go?" Ian asked me when he came home.

"It was wonderful," I replied smiling. "I should never have let it stop."

"I'm glad," said Ian looking relieved. "It's a much cheaper relaxation than going to the dentist."

Wendy Hamilton

Running Away.

"How about we run away," I suggested to my husband.

"We would have to take the kids with us," he replied pulling a face.

He was sitting on the kitchen floor with a howling toddler on one knee and a bawling baby on the other. His folded legs flailed up and down as he cheerily joggled his noisy burdens.

"Spoilsport. They are the reason I want to run away."

He did not answer me. Instead, he started singing loudly, "aren't we a happy little family?"

Many times, that man was the only thing that made my job palatable.

My mother was therapeutic too. No Madonna-with-amnesia words from her.

"Yes dear, it's just horrible. I remember the time I hid from you all in the closet. You went through the house shouting *Mum, Mum* and I kept very quiet. And do you remember the time I paid you kids fifty cents to go away?"

I Told You Not To Climb The Cactus

"Do you think they would go away if I paid them fifty cents each?" I asked Ian, jerking my head towards the foolish twaddle going on down the hallway.

"Don't worry Wend, you don't have to hide in the closet, I will take them all to the park for a couple of hours," he comforted me. He repositioned his howling burdens and stood up. "Marie," he called, "Get the big pram and the baby bag, we are going to the park."

"Can we feed the ducks?" asked Hannah running into the kitchen.

"Of course," said Ian.

"There are some old crusts in the bread bin," I said helpfully. (Anything to prolong the time they would be out of the house.)

There was a rattle and a bang as Marie wheeled the pram into the side of the doorframe.

"Be a bit more careful," I said, "you need to slow down through the doorways."

"Here we go, Bubba," said Ian laying Mark in the pram and tucking him in. He lifted a small seat onto the end of the pram and sat Joe on top. "Do you want to go walkies and feed the duckies Joe?" he asked brightly as he strapped him in. Like a dog, Joe perked up at the word walkies. He stopped blubbing and sucked his index and middle finger patiently.

"Wear your gumboots girls," I said, pulling a small red pair onto Joe's feet. "It has been raining so the park will be muddy around the pond."

"Where are they?" asked Marie.

"In the shoebox on the back porch where they live," I said irritably.

She ran out.

Wendy Hamilton

"I can't find them," she yelled a few minutes later.

I stomped out the back door and over to a wooden box with the word *Army* blazoned the side. "There they are, open your eyes," I said in exasperation, as I pulled out two pairs of gumboots.

Meanwhile, Hannah had liberally scattered crumbs over the kitchen floor in her quest for crusts. I ignored the mess because I did not want to delay their departure. It seemed to take forever but at last (after a few false starts) they were out the door and away. I quickly tidied the kitchen and added a few sticks of firewood to the wood-range, before pulling the kettle over the hot plate. The pleasure of a cup of tea in an empty house was unspeakably wonderful. I pulled the rocking chair close to the big black range and sat with my feet on the fender. It was so restful having the house all to myself. The silence, broken only by the whistle of the kettle, engulfed me like a warm comforting blanket. I filled the teapot leisurely, and when it was brewed I poured myself a cup of tea and sipped slowly. Two hours alone did wonders for me.

Sometimes, however, I needed much more than two hours. Fortunately, I had a bolt hole in the form of a tiny weekend cottage in the hills.

"I think you need to go to Mount Tiger by yourself this weekend," said Ian looking at me thoughtfully one Friday night.

"I feel too tired," I groaned. "It seems too much effort."

"Now I *know* you need to go," said Ian. "You can't keep functioning if you don't have a break, especially as you are home-schooling the girls."

"I feel a fraud. I don't seem to get much schooling done," I said morosely.

I Told You Not To Climb The Cactus

"That makes no difference," said Ian. "You still have them around you twenty-four-seven. It must be about six weeks since your last real break and I can tell you need the weekend off."

"How?"

"You're yelling more than usual and you haven't jumped at the opportunity to get them out of your hair."

"That is a tip-off," I agreed.

"Go now," said Ian bossily.

I needed him to be bossy. When my decision-making-powers got this low, he knew I needed pushing.

"I suppose so," I agreed listlessly.

"You could have Chinese takeaways for dinner," he added persuasively.

"Hmmm, yes I could," I said perking up at the idea. "In fact, I could get two huge pottles and not cook all weekend." The idea was growing.

"Just think, no children, only the misty clouds rising up from the valley and the hawks riding the thermal waves outside the bedroom window……All alone….. You don't even need to pack. You have a nighty and toothbrush out there and there is extra food in the cupboard. Think about it."

As he spoke desire kindled. A fight broke out at the other end of the house. The sound of squabbling kids suddenly fanned desire into a flame of activity. I grabbed my handbag and the keys to the van.

"See you on Sunday afternoon," I said to my marvelous husband as I kissed him goodbye.

Our little cottage, perched on the ridge of Mount Tiger, was a mere twenty-minute drive away. It was rustic, without electricity, and boasted only a rudimentary bathroom. The

Wendy Hamilton

view, however, was spectacular. I arrived with my steaming pottles of Chinese food as the twilight slid into darkness. I unlocked the door, lit the oil lamp, and ate Sweet and Sour Pork in a pool of yellow light.

I still hadn't worked out how to take my husband with me but I had managed to run away; and what's more, I never wanted to go back!

I went to bed and slept sixteen hours straight. The next day I lounged around, drank tea, read books, ate black-bean-beef-stew and went to bed early. The thought of returning to the bosom of my family made me shudder.

I awoke refreshed on Sunday morning. Only six hours left before I have to go back, I thought, counting my hours of reprieve like a miser counts gold. I made the most of it by lying in the sun and listening to the birds.

By lunchtime inevitably, a subtle change was creeping over me that had nothing to do with eating Chinese food, yet again. The birds were still nice and the sun was pleasant. A new thought, dim at first but growing in illumination, lit up my brain.

"If I did not have children and this was my life, it would be empty and meaningless," I said aloud.

Sunday afternoon was a joyful time, as rejuvenated, I locked up and drove home; humming all the way.

"Home sweet home," I said to the house as I parked the van in the garage.

The noise hit me before I opened the kitchen door. My faithful husband was sitting cross-legged on the floor bouncing a bawling baby on one knee and a howling toddler on the other. In the background, the distinctive sound of silly fooling floated down the hallway while Ian sang through gritted teeth, "aren't we a happy little family?"

I Told You Not To Climb The Cactus

I laughed, kissed him and agreed. Yes, we were a *very* happy little family. Life doesn't get better than this!

Wendy Hamilton

Life does not get much better than this.

I Told You Not To Climb The Cactus

About the Author

New Zealander Wendy Hamilton, was involved in homeschooling for over twenty years. She currently resides in Australia with her husband Ian and her four children. Wendy enjoys crafts, gardening, writing, and drawing.

Wendy Hamilton

Other Books By Wendy Hamilton

Darling the Window is on Fire

Eating a Light Bulb does not make you Bright.
Light on Home-schooling

Homemade Church

Children's Novels
The Britwhistles win a Prize
The Britwhistles and the Elasticizer

Children's Picture books
The Unlucky Snails
The Unlucky Snails go to France

These can be found at
www.zealauspublishing.com

www.ingramcontent.com/pod-product-compliance
Lightning Source LLC
Chambersburg PA
CBHW021104080526
44587CB00010B/375